DATE DUE

APR LIBRA 92			
MAR 1 8 1993			
JUL 0 9 2019			
GAYLORD			PRINTED IN U.S.A.

A CASEBOOK OF WITCHCRAFT

By the Same Author

Fiction

THE EDGE OF DARKNESS

THE STREET OF SEVEN MONKS

THE MASK

RIOT AT GRAVESEND

MANUELA

A MERMAID IN NIKOLI

Nonfiction

A YUGOSLAV ADVENTURE

POLAND: PHOENIX IN THE EAST

A HISTORY OF THE DEVIL

A CASEBOOK OF WITCHCRAFT

A CASEBOOK OF WITCHCRAFT

REPORTS, DEPOSITIONS, CONFESSIONS, TRIALS,
AND EXECUTIONS FOR WITCHCRAFT DURING
A PERIOD OF THREE HUNDRED YEARS

Selected and annotated by

WILLIAM *Howard* WOODS

Andrew S. Thomas Memorial Library
MORRIS HARVEY COLLEGE, CHARLESTON, W. VA.

G. P. PUTNAM'S SONS, NEW YORK

COPYRIGHT © 1974 BY WILLIAM WOODS

All rights reserved. This book, or parts thereof, must not be reproduced in any form without permission.

SBN: 399-11403-3

Library of Congress Catalog
Card 74-79672

"The Tariff for Torture in Cologne" taken from *The Encyclopedia of Witchcraft and Demonology* by Russell Hope Robbins.© 1959 by Crown Publishers, Inc., New York. Used by permission of Crown Publishers, Inc.

PRINTED IN THE UNITED STATES OF AMERICA

Contents

	INTRODUCTION	ix
1.	The Old Testament and the Saxon Kings	23
2.	The Witch of Endor	24
3.	Jonah and the Whale	27
4.	A Polynesian Jonah	27
5.	The Abbot Regino of Prüm	28
6.	The Bull of Innocent VIII	29
7.	How Witches Steal Away from Their Husbands	31
8.	Some Prescriptions for Flying Ointment	32
9.	A Gentlewoman at Lyons	33
10.	The Devil's Dinners	34
11.	A Succubus at Hemingen	34
12.	How the Devil Marries Young Women	36
13.	The Use of Dead Bodies to Make Magic	36
14.	A Child Sacrificed in Africa	38
15.	Obligatory Death of a Child in Africa	39
16.	Eating Salt During Pregnancy	39
17.	Unbaptized Infants Dug Up in Scotland	40
18.	Mme. de Montespan's Mass	40
19.	Killing Children to Cause Dissension	41
20.	A Witch Turns into a Dog	42
21.	The Torture of Father Dominic Gordel	42
22.	A Girl Discovers Her Mother's Witchcraft	47
23.	A Scottish Incubus	48
24.	Another Scot's Succubus Defeated	49
25.	A Husband Falls in Love with a Witch	50
26.	Reginald Scot Ridicules the Incubus	50
27.	How Children Are Infected with Witchcraft	52
28.	A Girl Betrays Her Mother as a Witch	53
29.	Midwives and Whores Who Murder Children	54

30.	Sorcerers in India	54
31.	Sickness and Death in the Congo	55
32.	Trial of the *Elamango*	55
33.	The Doomed Heretic of Cambrai	56
34.	The Adulterous Porter of Bassompierre	57
35.	Witches Attack Men's Masculinity	58
36.	Cures for Bewitchment of the Private Parts	60
37.	A Charm for the Toothache	61
38.	From the Trial of Joan of Arc	62
39.	A Barotse Joan of Arc	62
40.	A White Witch in Yorkshire	63
41.	Aboriginal Medicine with Quartz Crystals	65
42.	An Elephant Possessed of the Devil	66
43.	Congolese Evil Spirits	66
44.	The Abyssinian *Boudah*	66
45.	The Possession of Madeleine de la Palud	70
46.	The Tariff for Torture in Cologne	76
47.	Elspeth Reoch Meets the Devil	78
48.	Copulation with the Devil	79
49.	The Devil and Pacts with Children	80
50.	Reginald Scot on the Sabbat	81
51.	Love Magic in Kamtchatka	82
52.	The Deposition of Silvain Neuillon	82
53.	Induction of Children into the Sabbat	87
54.	Young Witches Love the Devil	88
55.	Witches and Dancing	89
56.	William Barton's Succubus and Death	90
57.	Witches in North Berwick	92
58.	Feasting with the Devil	93
59.	A Great Meeting in Loudian	93
60.	Elizabeth Gowdie's Horse and Hattock	94
61.	Ann Armstrong Ridden by Witches	94

62.	The Devil in Wales	95
63.	John Fian's Love Magic Foiled	96
64.	The Confession of Agnes Simpson	99
65.	The Confession of Agnes Thompson	100
66.	The Torture and Death of John Fian	101
67.	The Death of Janet Cornfoot in Pittenweem	102
68.	The Pied Piper of Hamlen	103
69.	Scot on Witches' Confessions	104
70.	A Gallows Dialogue with Three Witches	106
71.	The Eyebiting Witches of Ireland	111
72.	Simon Davie's Bewitched Wife	112
73.	Scot on Witchcraft as Superstition	114
74.	Death for Witchcraft in Angola	116
75.	Witchcraft in Papua	116
76.	The Basuto Ordeal by Boiling Water	117
77.	A Scapegoat Among the A-Kamba	117
78.	A Man and his Wife Murdered for Witchcraft	118
79.	The Bewitching of John Tonken	118
80.	A Drunkard Bewitched in Royston	119
81.	Twelve African Women Accused of Witchcraft	121
82.	Jane Brooks Hanged for Witchcraft	122
83.	Julian Cox and Her Toad	127
84.	A Maori Lizard in the Path	127
85.	*Atua* in New Zealand	128
86.	The Drummer of Tedworth	128
87.	The Examination of Christian Green	144
88.	Image Witchcraft Among Australian Aborigines	149
89.	The Ordeal of the Old Man of Mpete	149
90.	Eighteen Witches Drowned in the Congo	150
91.	The Deposition of Elizabeth Style	150

92.	Florence Newton Unable to Pray	161
93.	A Cast of the Bones in South Africa	162
94.	Casting the Bones in the Transvaal	162
95.	The American Indian Shaman	163
96.	East and West African *Muavi*	163
97.	False Accusation and Death in Stockholm	165
98.	The Witches of Blockula	165
99.	An African Chief Condemns his Mother	176
100.	Thirty-one Dead Wives in Africa	176
101.	The Confessions at Paisley	177
102.	Disease Is Supernatural in Polynesia	181
103.	"God and I Are Equal"	182
104.	John Goodwin's Children in Salem	183
105.	Goody Glover Condemns Herself	185
106.	Examination of Elizabeth Procter in Salem	186
107.	An Appeal from Salem Prison	189
108.	Testimony Against Bridget Bishop	190
109.	Death Warrant of Bridget Bishop	194
110.	From the Examination of George Jacobs	195
111.	From the Examination of Sarah Good	196
112.	Nathaniel Cary Attends his Wife's Hearing	198
113.	Ann Putnam and Goody Corey	201
114.	The Deposition of Ann Putnam	203
115.	The Deposition of Sarah Ingersoll	206
116.	Goody Tyler's Evidence to Increase Mather	207
117.	Mary Easty's Appeal before Hanging	208
118.	The Hearing of John Alden, Mariner	209
119.	The Afflictions of Margaret Rule	211
120.	The Salem Jury's Apology	214
121.	Ann Putnam's Confession from the Pulpit	216

Introduction

THIS CASEBOOK deals with interesting but very complex matters, with a history that is half fact and half hearsay, with things that happened or were said to have happened before the rules of evidence or even the limits of credulity had been more than cursorily laid down.

And the evidence suffers not only this handicap. Those who reported the history were all biased, and biased in the same direction. They were indignant, righteous, ignorant, and frightened men; the very roots of their faith had been questioned or denied. Their whole sanctimoniously built system of hierarchies, of reason and causality, had been laid open to doubt, and they lacked what we should call the scientific logic or rationality with which they might have defended themselves. Superstition they countered with superstition, magic with magic, and since the very foundations of their Christian establishment were being undermined, they responded at last with a blind rage that damaged the very principles they were trying to uphold. A frightened man is all the more dangerous when he has only an uncertain idea what has actually attacked him.

So we have to begin by defining not so much who these men were, but what they feared. Now, Margaret Murray, in her *The Witch Cult in Western Europe* and in *The God of the Witches* produced some remarkable evidence for the assertion that witchcraft was nothing but the relic of a much older what she calls a *vecchia religione,* an animistic and amoral awareness of the interaction, the interrelationship, between man and the inanimate universe with which he was surrounded.

The modern sense for ecology touches no more than the fringe of it. I have pointed out elsewhere that the animist's world (and we shall hear many echoes of it in this volume) was crowded not only with the spirits of tangible objects, of trees, plants, artifacts, and particular places, but with those of active invisible powers too, the ghosts of his ancestors, of his enemies, and of a host of lesser demons that had to be identified, cajoled, and propitiated. We are still aware today of some of the intangible powers that overawed him, the magic of iron and salt, the interaction of objects resembling one another, the holiness of springs and "wishing wells," the efficacy of charms, the prophetic quality of dreams, the quite un-understandable power to move us of sunrise and sunset, midsummer, midwinter and the equinoxes. A simple fear of the dark and the fears that oppress some of us in the "dead, vast middle of the night" are nothing but shadowy reminders of the fear that haunted us perpetually during hundreds of similar centuries, during which no practical causes for events were even so much as suspected, and no reasonable effects of one's actions could ever be foretold.

It can be demonstrated that all Western religions and almost all of our current superstitions originated in that dark, vivid, endlessly frightening world before history began to be written—when health, sickness, the seasons, when natural phenomena like rain or drought, hail, thunder, fire were as immediate to a man as his own fingertips, when he bore them so intimate a relationship, felt for them so jumbled a love and fear, when they and he so interacted that he studied by every means in his power both to understand them and to bend them to his uses.

To go a step further, anthropologists have demonstrated beyond question that he did not think as we should think—logically—about these things. There was—and this is difficult for us to understand—no causality in what happened. The tree did not fall because the wind blew it down. It fell because its spirit had been traduced, bewitched if you like, by the enemy of the man it fell on. A man never died because of sickness or a wound. He died because an object deliberately fashioned to resemble him was wounded or made sick, because a malevolent thought had taken away his protective spirits, because in slightly more modern terms, the devil had traduced his guardian angel.

We can go further still into this animate inanimate. Salt has the power to preserve meat. It could therefore just as rationally seal a bargain, a friendship, a marriage. A man who ate salt in your house could feel himself safe. Or take the miracle of iron. It fell as thunderbolts, was obviously the gift of the gods, and it revolutionized warfare. Practically speaking, it could be forged into terrible new weapons of which more primitive peoples were afraid. But its magic lay not in its practical uses; its magic lay in its having a spirit that gave it a supernatural, a godlike quality. In the twentieth century some of us still wear iron rings to cure diseases, and as modern an Englishman as Charles Dickens slept with his bed lying north and south because he imagined beneficial effects to himself of thus using the earth's magnetic force on his own body.

If there were powers one could enlist to help, there were multitudes of others that had either to be bought off with sacrifices, or at least worshiped so they would do one no harm. And the chief of these malevolent ones was the great horned god of one's ancestors. He had been born to the paleolithic hunter who painted representations of him in a hundred caves. He was the magic-inducing figure of the animal-in-man, the mutually interrelated spirit that helped one by identifying oneself with the animal, to succeed in the hunt.

That this figure was originally no more than that of a man wearing a stag's antlers seems obvious enough. That eventually the image became a worker of magic is no more than a logical next step. And from this to being adored, propitiated, prayed to is simply the fate of all magic-bearing bodies. The devout who pray to a statue of the Virgin are doing something remarkably similar. For them, image and object become one; the image, like that of the doomed primitive, has been deliberately fashioned to resemble its prototype. What the statue hears, the Virgin will hear. What the image of the man suffers, the man himself will suffer.

But in a word, with the advent of Christianity, this simple, awesome, and necessary horned god became the devil. Here, in a nutshell, we have the *vecchia religione*. The gambler at dice who "conjures the bones," the child who plays at not stepping on cracks in the pavement, the poet who sets down sometimes magical associative images off the top of his head, the racetrack tout who has a system, the astrologist, the dowser for water, the breaker of wishbones, and the interpreter of dreams all have this thing in common, that they are ignoring our experience of causality and perhaps unwittingly practicing a religion older than Jesus. Sometimes, astonishing as it may seem, they are not unjustified.

Now, the witchcraft of sixteenth- and seventeenth-century Europe and America was apparently a much debased example of this old religion. Its practitioners danced with the devil in human form, feasted, made music, and copulated with him, adored him, and with his help tried to do harm to their enemies. Who these devils were we have no way of knowing, except that they are described so often and in such similar detail that there can be no doubt at all but that they existed. In France, in Sweden, and particularly in Scotland people talk about them in terms that might almost be echoes one of another. The devil may be young or old, but he generally wears black. His voice is "rough" or "low and gusty." Sometimes his feet are cloven. But almost always he is a great lover of women. His penis is large and painful to accept, his semen cold as ice. And if he is a pure figment of the imagination, it seems odd that so many imaginations were alike, and that the dream was vivid enough to induce witches very often to go almost joyously to their deaths.

Sometimes the devil assumes an almost recognizable shape. Elspeth Reoch (No. 47) is seduced by a devil who is a "fairy man," and the fairy man is a figure we know. Our Iron Age ancestors drove their more primitive neighbors into the forests, and there these people lived on for centuries in mound dwellings almost indistinguishable from the surrounding vegetation. They were small, swift, dark (a different race, in fact), and it seems fairly evident that they survived in England and western Europe well into the seventeenth century. They were said to have a great knowledge of herbs, both for poisoning and for curing sickness, and I have no real doubt that the white witch in Yorkshire (No. 40) had been taught some of their magic.

In these pages we shall meet the devil in a variety of times and places and doing a variety of things. He preaches, he presides at the Sabbat, he plots murder with his followers and punishes the recalcitrant among them. But above all, he gives those who adore him a pleasure so intense (and not only sexual) that Mme. Bourignon's orphans, for example, reported themselves as being unwilling ever to change. In one of our excerpts (No. 54) young women tell their inquisitor that they attend the devil's meetings with "a mad delight," and will gladly die if dying means they may be with him forevermore.

"Jesus is in heaven," he has told them, "but I am here and can help you." And of course by our lights it was a drab and monotonous world they lived in. But that devil gave them not only variety but a pleasure they could never hope to find anywhere else. More important, he was part of a religion preternaturally acceptable because it was a piece of folk memory, of what Jung has called the *a priori* that underlies everything we most easily believe.

That religion, if we can call it such, has actually survived almost unaltered into the twentieth century. Philippe Alfonsi and Patrick Pesnot spent two years recently investigating a very similar witchcraft in modern France, and their findings make quite plain how little has really changed in five hundred years. "If we had wished," Pesnot writes, "we could have made the same inquiry in the Limousin or the Vendee or the Sarthe regions, for hundreds of police reports exist in these districts of similar manifestations."*

What they found was neither a relic of folklore nor even part of the fashionable occult revival. They talked to peasants in Berry, near Bourges, and found that they had walked into a world where magic is still a vitally important part of everyday thinking. As in every peasant community, simple accidents, family quarrels, rumor, gossip run like dark threads through almost every man's life, and in Berry, just as in the long dead pagan communities, those accidents, those quarrels and misfortunes are ascribed to a witchcraft endemic almost in the soil. Saints were "good ones" or "bad ones." Formulas for curing diseases were collected out of old treatises on magic and written down in blood.

The authors tell us that "When a peasant sees his farm begin to run down, and his worries keep him awake or make him ill, he is immediately convinced that somebody has cast a spell on him. The spell-breaker he consults only confirms his

---

*Philippe Alfonsi and Patrick Pesnot, *L'Oeil du Sorcier* (Paris, 1973).

suspicions. He won't, to be sure, give the peasant the name of his persecutor, only the means to discover who it is. There are several ways to do this. It might be sufficient to make the sign of the cross in the street. The first person to turn round is the witch.

"When a spell is put on a farm or its inhabitants," they write, "it is usually because somebody wants to buy the place. And when that happens, one has only to look round at the neighbours to see who is most likely to profit. The first person who makes an offer is the *j'teux d'sorts,* the caster of spells, and the offer has been a proof of his diabolic intentions."

But now the peasant knows who his enemy is. He has become able to put a face to evil, a voice. He knows where it lives. It is not his method of farming that is at fault, or the laws of economics. The field turned sour, the cow died, the barn caught fire, not because of any fault of his own, but because of a neighbor's malevolence. Now he can sleep easy, for now he knows where the counterattack must be directed. Witchcraft has acquired a pragmatic face, and become as much part of the casual consciousness as it must have done five hundred years ago. It is only when this much has been accomplished, says Roger-Pol Droit (writing in *Le Monde*), "it is then and then only that active witchcraft begins, the sticking of pins into photographs, the reciting of magic formulae, sometimes even sacrifices."

Nobody, he points out, nobody in this localized peasant war works evil for evil's sake. It is always somebody else who started it. "The figure of the malevolent dabbler in black magic, the devil's henchman, fills an essential mythical function. You never actually meet him, but he is always there, and belief in his existence justifies whatever you do in your own defence."

It has been said that in matters of faith, God wrote all the books. In matters of witchcraft, in the history of witchcraft, the books were written by judges and ecclesiastics. And these were angry men because they were part of the establishment, and the establishment had discarded with an active loathing what it felt to be not only the un-Christian but the irrational past.

Not only this. In the recital of all these tales out of the

fifteenth, the sixteenth, and the seventeenth centuries, the establishment was indignant because it was faced with a mystique and a joy that seemed not only directed against all it stood for, but with ways of reasoning entirely outside its control. Unlike the religion of Jews or Moslems, the *vecchia religione* was not only the enemy of God. Its followers were enemies of learning, enemies of commerce, enemies of morality, enemies of what all decent people took to be acceptable standards of behavior. So with the divine anger of the righteous, the judges and inquisitors not only punished. They subjected their suspects to what seem now incredible tortures. Pierre de Lancre insisted that those he had condemned be not strangled before they were burned so that their torments might last all the longer. Nicholas Remy passed like an avenging angel through Lorraine and had some nine hundred sent to the stake in the space of fifteen years. In England torture was prohibited, but in Scotland confessions were normally pulled out of unwilling throats on the rack, and the inquisitors who condemned Louis Gauffridi were not satisfied with burning him alive. They ordered that in front of the stake he first be subjected to the *question extraordinaire,* so that he might suffer such excruciating tortures that the flames would come almost as a relief.

Many, probably by far the greater number of confessions, were extracted in this way, and we can therefore not rely on them for evidence of what suspects had actually done. Even the similarity of these confessions from places as far apart as the highlands of Scotland and the Basque Pyrenees lends no particular weight to the depositions. For the judges had read the *Malleus Maleficarum* of Sprenger and Kramer, that great fifteenth-century compendium of cases brought before the Holy Office in Germany. They knew what to expect. They knew what they wanted to hear, and the torture often did not cease until it had evoked whatever corroborative detail they needed to fill these expectations.

But even when this is granted there is a residue of truth in the accounts that cannot be denied. Here and threre we find the unexpected detail that seems unlikely to have been invented. There is the candle, for example, that went "wig wag, wig wag" in the devil's tail (No. 56), the image magic in Paisley (No. 101), the remarkable similarity of women's experience in copulating with the devil (No. 48), and above all the evident and often expressed joy experienced in the devil's sacraments; these are not the sorts of things one expects to hear from the rack. So we have to face the fact that there was a society of old religionists, a positive flood of little societies, and that we are never likely to know more about them than we do today.

So far as I know, not one document belonging to the witches themselves has survived. Perhaps the documents never existed. As I pointed out earlier, the evidence comes solely from the prosecutors, and prosecutors are generally blind in one eye. Even a cursory glance at their evidence reveals that they often did not even know what enemy they were trying to attack. Heretics, political dissidents, common criminals, and a host of maundering old women were all caught in the same net. The most reliable estimates suggest that in the course of three hundred years they executed about nine million people in the name of Christian orthodoxy. How many of these were practitioners of the old religion we cannot tell.

But an anti-Christian religion there was, and most of the evidence for it is here set down in roughly chronological order. From a variety of sources, described more fully in the text, I have chosen excerpts to give as rounded a picture as I can of the various activities in which witches unquestionably indulged. Some of the accounts are more than hearsay, or the results of torture. The story of Father Dominic Gordel (No. 21) is the simple stenographic report of what happened to him on the rack and what he said. The story of Madeleine de la Palud, her possession and exorcism during a period of many months (No. 45) is taken from the statement of her inquisitor, Sebastian Michaelis, who was of course present at the time. The dialogue at the gallows (No. 70) is also a verbatim account, and here I should like to interject a word of advice. It ought not be read as a simple series of questions and answers. One must first picture to oneself the confused old women on the brink of death. There they stand in front of the Reverend Mr. Hann, confused, hesitant, frightened and unsure even of what is being asked.

"How did you know it was the devil?"

Here one ought to supply the pause for thought, the uncertain glance from hangman to priest, from accomplice to the gaping audience.

"I knew it by his eyes."

Or, to take another part of the same interrogation:

"Was it you or Susan that did bewitch the children?"

A simple question, requiring a simple answer. But the answer is not simple at all.

"I sold apples," she says, "and the child took an apple from me. And the mother took the apple from the child, for the which I was very angry." Then the long pause before she adds, "But the child died of the small pox."

How much is left unsaid! How much of the scene has to be supplied by the imagination!

On the other hand, there is very little indeed left to the imagination in the long accounts from Glanvill. Here was an earnest eighteenth-century cleric, a learned man, a thoroughly honest, but much bemused man setting down depositions taken by country magistrates, depositions made without torture as he explicitly informs us, but containing matter he simply could not understand. How was he to know (No. 82) that young Richard Jones was probably suffering from epilepsy, and that it was the boy's inexplicable illness, not any crime of Jane Brooks, that caused her to be hanged? His drummer of Tedworth (No. 86), on the other hand, is one of the classic poltergeist stories, one of many hundreds, and no more explainable today than it was when he set it down.

The last eighteen excerpts come from Salem, Massachusetts, in 1692, and what can one say of them except that they are perhaps the most moving of all? For these people and what they suffered seem almost part of our immediate past. We recognize them. They are not ignorant rustics practicing an old religion, but they are contaminated by it. And in spite of that contamination they are our American neighbors, as familiar as blueberry pie.

Much has been written about Ann Putnam's possession and subsequent recantation. Whether or not she and her friends were really "possessed" we cannot know, but what happened at the house of Lieutenant Ingersoll (No. 106) may provide at least part of the answer. In any case, they hanged the Reverend George Burroughs. Whether or not Margaret Rule was actually levitated out of her bed (No. 119) as six separate witnesses deposed we cannot know either. But one bit of medical evidence we do have. My friend, Derek Wilson, a physician, has read the reports and he points out that John Louder (No. 108) was quite clearly suffering from angina pectoris owing to myocardial ischemia and that from this feeling of stricture in the chest came his illusion that a witch sat on his chest at night. On the basis of his further evidence the man was simply drunk and had had an attack of delirium tremens.

"I not being very well," he says, "stayed at home on a Lord's Day." A simple statement. But as with the old women on the gallows, we have to read between the lines. "Not being very well," he saw not a pink elephant, but a black pig in the room. And the pig was quite clearly the devil. Later he "struck at" a thing "with a stick, but struck the groundsill and broke the stick, and that arm with which I struck was presently disenabled." So Bridget Bishop who had supposedly sat on his chest at night had subsequently to be hanged.

In a word, we may fairly conclude that a sizable proportion of the accused in all ages were probably not actually guilty of the crimes for which they died. At worst, they may have been malevolent and tried to conjure some enemy dead, wished like Margaret Agar (No. 87) to tread on a man's jaws, as she had already done (she said) on several occasions. So would some of the rest of us if only we dared. At best they brewed love philters, and who at least in his imagination has not done the same? And how many jilted girls have not wished they knew a charm that would revenge them by making their lovers impotent? How many of us have not dreamed we could fly?

All this is rationally to be explained. But the wishful thinking aside, there were not inconsiderable numbers, not of old hags but of vigorous men and handsome young women, and these practiced a magic (or what they thought of as magic) that they felt in their very blood and bones to be valid, just as the magic of twentieth-century Berry is felt to be valid. It had been handed down from parent to child for over two thousand years.

So the whole gamut of witchlike activities for which there is any serious evidence is here set down. Interspersed with these European accounts are several shorter ones from India, from the South Seas, from various parts of Africa and pre-Christian America, and I have included these so that there may be no real question how widespread the old animistic religion was in the world.

The purpose of this short anthology is to draw an outline of the facts, and to do so as coherently as I can without deviating from the sources and without making the story interminable. Whoever would like to know more will find many of the available sources here described.

But the pity of it is that we shall never actually know any *more.* We may simply find more evidence. But even the little we have seems to me intensely valuable because the best history should not be so much the record of what has happened as of the changing human condition.

So here is some part of the record, a record now almost entirely submerged, first by a doctrinaire Christianity, and latterly by an industrialization that has already more than half buried both the real world and the very human roots from which we grew.

WILLIAM WOODS

Glascwm,
Radnorshire
11 September 1973

A CASEBOOK OF WITCHCRAFT

It is a moot question whether maledictions against witches arose out of Mosaic law or out of a desire in the religious and secular authorities of the early Middle Ages to stamp out the visible remnants of a primitive religion which in some parts of Sicily and in many of our own superstitions have not died even today. In a word, witchcraft has no recognizable beginnings. There have always been clairvoyants and necromancers, people who thought themselves (or at least their spiritual leaders) able to do magic. We long to foreknow what will come or, by some intangible and irrational means, to affect what is already here. From the very beginnings there have been men and women who claimed to be able to do both. But because the authorities could rarely do either, they invariably used such men and women whenever they felt the need (William, the Conqueror bought witches, and Hitler, an astrologer), or when they could not use them, prevented their possible use by anyone else.

1. The Old Testament and the Saxon Kings

Thou shalt not suffer a witch to live.
—*Exodus* xxii. 18

Regard not them that have familiar spirits, neither seek after wizards to be defiled by them.
—*Leviticus* xix. 31

A man also or woman that hath a familiar spirit or that is a wizard shall surely be put to death: they shall stone them with stones: their blood shall be upon them.
—*Leviticus* xx. 27

And when they shall say unto you, Seek unto them that have familiar spirits, and unto wizards that peep and that mutter, should not a people seek unto their God?
—*Isaiah* viii. 19

Not only celebrating feasts in the abominable temples of the heathen is evil, and offering food there, but also accepting it. So is serving such hidden idolatry, having relinquished Christ. If at the kalends of January anyone go about dressed as a stag or a bull, thus turning himself into an

23

animal, put on the skin of a herd beast, or dress himself in the head of such a beast; anyone who in such manner clothe himself like a beast shall suffer penance for three years, for it is a diabolical act.

—THEODORE, *Archbishop of Canterbury* (668-690)

We demand that every priest zealously promote Christianity and totally extinguish every manifestation of heathenism, that he forbid worship at wells, necromancy, divination and enchantment, the vain practices carried on with spells, with elder trees and various other trees, and with stones. We demand that on feast days heathen songs and the devil's games be abstained from.

—*Laws of King Edgar*, 959

We rigorously forbid every heathenism. Heathenism is the worship of idols, of heathen gods, of the sun, the moon, fire, rivers, wells, stones and trees of the forest, no matter of what kind. Heathenism is the love of witchcraft.

—*Laws of King Canute*, 1017-1035

* * *

The Witch of Endor has become a byword, an old hag in a smoky cavern. She is the earliest individualized witch of whom we have record. But there is no evidence that she was either old or ugly or malevolent. Quite the contrary. Her cottage had an earthen floor, but there was a bed fit for a king to sit on. She was hospitable, thoughtful, and she could actually do what she promised. She could raise the dead. The story is told in I Samuel xxviii. 3-25.

2. The Witch of Endor

Now Samuel was dead, and all Israel had lamented him and buried him in Ramah, even in his own city. And Saul had put away those that had familiar spirits and the wizards out of the land.

And the Philistines gathered themselves together and

came and pitched in Shunem. And Saul gathered all Israel together, and they pitched in Gilbus. And when Saul saw the host of the Philistines he was afraid, and his heart greatly troubled. And when Saul enquired of the Lord, the Lord answered him not, neither by dreams, nor by Urim, nor by the prophets.

Then said Saul unto his servants, Seek me a woman that hath a familiar spirit that I may go to her and enquire of her. And his servants said to him, Behold, there is a woman that hath a familiar spirit at Endor. And Saul disguised himself and put on other raiment, and he went and two men with him, and they came to the woman by night. And he said, I pray thee, divine unto me by the familiar spirit, and bring me him up whom I shall name unto thee.

And the woman said unto him, Behold, thou knowest what Saul hath done, how he hath cut off those that have familiar spirits and the wizards out of the land. Wherefore then layest thou a snare for my life, to cause me to die?

And Saul sware to her by the Lord, saying, as the Lord liveth there shall no punishment happen to thee for this thing. Then said the woman, Whom shall I bring up unto thee? And he said, Bring me up Samuel.

And when the woman saw Samuel she cried out with a loud voice. And the woman spake to Saul, saying, Why hast thou deceived me, for thou art Saul? And the king said unto her, Be not afraid; for what sawest thou? And the woman said unto Saul, I saw gods ascending out of the earth. And he said unto her, What form is he of? And she said, An old man cometh up, and he is covered with a mantle. And Saul perceived that it was Samuel, and he stooped with his face to the ground and bowed himself.

And Samuel said to Saul, Why hast thou disquieted me to bring me up? And Saul answered, I am sore distressed, for the Philistines make war against me, and God is departed from me and answereth me no more, neither by prophets, nor by dreams. Therefore I have called thee that thou mayest make known unto me what I shall do.

Then said Samuel, Wherefore then dost thou ask of me, seeing the Lord is departed from thee and is become thine enemy? And the Lord hath done to him as he spake by me, for the Lord hath rent the kingdom out of thine hand and given it to thy neighbour, even to David. Because thou obeyest not the voice of the Lord, or executedst his fierce wrath upon Amalek, therefore hath the Lord done this thing unto thee this day.

Moreover the Lord will also deliver Israel with thee into the hand of the Philistines, and tomorrow shalt thou and thy sons be with me. The Lord also shall deliver the host of Israel into the hands of the Philistines.

Then Saul fell straightway all along the earth and was sore afraid because of the words of Samuel, and there was no strength in him. For he had eaten no bread all the day, nor all the night.

And the woman came unto Saul and saw that he was sore troubled, and said unto him, Behold, thine handmaid hath obeyed thy voice, and I have put my life in my hand and have hearkened unto thy words which thou spakest unto me. Now therefore I pray thee, hearken thou also unto the voice of thine handmaid and let me set a morsel of bread before thee, and eat that thou mayest have strength when thou goest on thy way. But he refused and said, I will not eat. But his servants together with the woman compelled him, and he hearkened unto their voice.

So he arose from the earth and sat upon the bed. And the woman had a fat calf in the house, and she hasted and killed it, and took flour and kneaded it, and did bake unleavened bread thereof. And she brought it before Saul and before his servants, and they did eat. Then they rose up and went away that night.

* * *

> But witchcraft was more than raising the dead. It was magic. It was sacrifice, and it was propitiation old as thunder. Under certain conditions, that is, and the story is recounted in a hundred shapes, from that of Iphigenia, who died to raise a wind, to that of many gods who died to rescue the harvest. The story in Jonah i. 11-15 is familiar to all of us.

3. Jonah and the Whale

Then said they unto him, What shall we do unto thee that the sea may be calm unto us? For the sea wrought and was tempestuous. And he said unto them, Take me up and cast me forth into the sea, so shall the sea be calm unto you, for I know that for my sake this great tempest is upon you. Nevertheless the men rowed hard to bring it to land, but they could not, for the sea wrought and was tempestous against them.

Wherefore they cried unto the Lord, and said, We beseech thee, let us not perish for this man's life, and lay not upon us innocent blood. For thou, O Lord, hast done as it pleased thee.

So they took up Jonah and cast him forth into the sea, and the sea ceased from her raging.

4. A Polynesian Jonah

A canoe with half a dozen men on board sailed from Aitutaki to Manuae (Hervey's Island), a distance of fifty five miles, in order to collect red parrakeets' feathers. Having succeeded in their object . . . they started on their return voyage, but were driven out of their course by strong contrary winds. After a few days food and water began to fail, and a miserable death stared them in the face. Routu, the commander of the canoe, now addressed his companions. "I see why we are thus driven about over the ocean by unfavourable winds. We have sinned in taking away the red parrakeets' feathers. A costly sacrifice is demanded by the angry gods. Throw me into the sea, and you will yet safely reach home." The voyagers . . . complied with the request.
—W.W. GILL, *Savage Life in Polynesia*

* * *

About the year 906 a certain Regino, Abbot of Prüm, near Trier, wrote down or caused to be written down a document which became known in time as the Canon Episcopi, *wherein certain women are castigated, not for what they have done, but for their too vivid imaginations and perhaps for what they would like to have done. Almost entirely on the basis of this pronouncement the church held for several hundred years that women rode out at night on certain beasts or on dildo broomsticks (we shall see eventually that the whole thing had great sexual significance) to meet their master, Satan. What is more important, it deluded certain women into believing that they had actually done so. On this canon the whole paraphernalia of seventeenth-century persecution of witches was originally based.*

5. The Abbot Regino of Prüm

Certain wicked women won over by the devil and seduced by illusions and hallucinations of demons believe and indeed state openly that they ride out at night with Diana, the pagan goddess. Countless numbers of these women travel vast distances in the dark, though it is only on certain nights that they are called out to do this service. If only they were destroyed by their own lack of faith! But no. Instead, they drag down many others into their own state of impiety. For they believe that a thing divine both in nature and in power can exist apart from the one true God. The clergy ought to preach that these are only demonic fancies put into their heads, not by God, but by the evil spirit. In this way Satan, who can take the shape of an angel, once he has tangled up some woman's wits, leads her astray in her dreams, so that the victim believes that what happened only in her imagination actually took place in the body.

* * *

On the 9th of December, 1484, Pope Innocent VIII (Giovanni Battista Cibo, 1432-92) issued his famous bull, Summis desiderantes affectibus, *and although papal pronouncements about witchcraft had been made by many of his predecessors, this was the first to achieve widespread circulation, for it was printed in the infamous* Malleus Maleficarum (The Hammer of Witches) *of Heinrich Kramer and Jacobus Sprenger, two Dominicans who had been appointed therein to hunt down and punish witchcraft in Germany. "It rang the tocsin against this formidable crime," Sir Walter Scott wrote, and it initiated a persecution which in time and with almost unparalleled savagery was to torture and destroy many hundreds of thousands of victims. Two years after the publication of the* Malleus, *Cibo appointed the notorious Tomas Torquemada inquisitor-general in Spain. As for the book that became the memorial of his antiheretical passion, the Reverend Montague Summers pointed out that "For nearly three centuries the Malleus lay on the bench of every judge, on the desk of every magistrate. It was the ultimate, the irrefutable authority." As for Innocent VIII, if he (one trusts, unwittingly) created for so many the ultimate reality in hell on earth, he seems to have been curiously anxious to postpone his own sight of the reality of heaven, for in the last months of his life he sucked a woman's breasts to get nourishment when he could take little other, and had blood pumped out of young boys' veins into his own until three of the boys died. One of his own children (and he had several) married a daughter of Lorenzo de' Medici.*

6, The Bull of Innocent VIII

It has come to our attention—and with bitter sorrow—that in some parts of northern Germany, particularly in the provinces, towns, districts and dioceses of Mainz, Cologne, Trier, Salzburg and Bremen, many persons of both sexes, unmindful of salvation and deviating from the Catholic faith, have abandoned themselves to devils, to incubi and succubi, and by their incantations, spells, conjurations and other accursed charms and crafts, enormities and horrid offences, have slain infants yet in the mother's womb, as also the offspring of cattle, have blasted the produce of the earth, the grapes of the vine, the fruits of trees, nay, men and women, beasts of burden, herd-beasts as well as animals of other kinds, vineyards, orchards, meadows, pasture land, corn, wheat and all other cereals: these wretches furthermore afflict and torment men and women as well as animals of other kinds with terrible and piteous pains and sore diseases, both internal and external; they hinder men from performing the sexual act and women from conceiving, whence husbands cannot know their wives nor wives receive their husbands; over and above this, they blasphemously renounce the Faith which is theirs by the sacrament of baptism, and at the instigation of the Enemy of Mankind they do not shrink from committing and perpetrating the foulest excesses to the deadly peril of their own souls, whereby they outrage the Divine Majesty and are a cause of scandal and danger to very many.

* * *

Nicholas Remy (Remigius) was born in 1530 in Charmes, just southeast of Nancy. Old and laden with honors, he died there in April, 1612. As a child he had watched witches being tried, for his father had been Provost of Charmes (Lorraine was a hotbed of witchcraft), and at the age of sixty-one he himself became Lord High Justice of Lorraine. In that post (as he says himself) he condemned some nine hundred witches to death in the course of fifteen years. He married a woman of some character and by her had at least seven children (the last born when he was sixty-eight). During term time he lived in Nancy, but during the holidays retired to his country house at Saint Mard near Bayon, where he gave himself up to his chief avocations, the study of literature and the writing of poetry, both French and Latin. In 1595 his Demonolatry *appeared, a summary of and commentary on some of the confessions he had heard during his many years on the bench, and it bears witness not only to his elegance and his learning, but as he would have said himself, to the cold logicality with which he examined whatever phenomena came to his attention. "Whatever is unknown or irrational," he wrote, "belongs in the accursed territory of demonology. A fact is never unexplainable. Whatever is abnormal, whatever is not a clearly explicable fact is the devil's work."* Urbane, erudite, ruthless, cruel, and credulous, Remy's work is one of the landmarks in any study of European witchcraft, not only for the stories it tells, but for the light it throws on the sixteenth-century mind that could not only accept those stories as factual, but could draw them like so many teeth—often with quite unimaginable tortures—out of the mouths of prisoners that had been brought to trial.

That there were witches in Lorraine goes without question. The evidence is voluminous, corroborative and rational. That many of these witches tried without any knowledge of causality to take revenges, get money, cause and cure sicknesses, and indeed, in an age when divorce was both legally and theologically impossible, to find covert sexual gratification seems equally clear. But unless one accepts that they could actually do magic, they were innocent of all but wishful thinking. We shall hear something of the Sabbat later, and of what actually took place there. But the Demonolatry *is not so much a record of fact as a record of what Remy and his contemporaries believed, wished to believe, or simply dreaded as they did the Devil himself.*

7. How Witches Steal Away from Their Husbands

The confessions of certain witches in Forbach in Lorraine have just come to my notice, and from these I have learned for the first time just how witches manage to steal out of their marriage beds when they wish to attend meetings. To keep their husbands from noticing any change in their usual habits they cast certain spells to make the men fall into a deep sleep. Or else they place something that looks and feels like their own bodies in the bed. Bertrande Barbier confessed that she had often done this. On several occasions when she wanted to make her husband sleep soundly, she had taken (in her right hand) some of the ointment used for flying, rubbed it on his right ear, and then (to test the potion) pinched him to see if he would wake. Eller, wife of an officer in Ottingen, had simply slipped a child's pillow into her place. Sinchen May of Speirchen used twigs for the same purpose after she had first called on her demon for help. Thus they all were betrayers of their husbands. Maria, wife of Johann Schneider in Metzereth, used a bundle of straw greased with her ointment, and invariably, as soon as she herself got safely home again, it disappeared. But according to Catherine Ruffa, it was the devil himself who took her place in bed.

—*Demonolatry*, I. xii

* * *

Reginald Scot (1538-99) had really only two interests, hop gardens and the unmasking of imposture. The one he treated as befitted a Kentish country gentleman. The other made a big, rational, mocking, civilized, and highly readable book that tried to put down the superstitious dread of witches with which most of his contemporaries were infected. James I called his Discoverie of Witchcraft *"a damnable book." Casaubon called its author "an illiterate wretch." And yet the* Discoverie *was one of the first real attempts to be rational about a highly irrational subject. Even when he seems credulous, Scot's tongue is at least partly in his cheek. He believed in powdered unicorn's horn as a cure for disease. But when he supplies a recipe for ointment to help one fly (as in our first excerpt) he is simply reporting what he has been told. When he tells the story of the witch of Lyons he thinks it rather funny. When he writes (as we shall see later) about a woman who had sold her soul to the devil, he offers a rational explanation without which the woman might very well have been hanged.*

8. Some Prescriptions for Flying Ointment

Rx. The fat of yoong children, and seeth it with water in a brasen vessell, reserving the thickest of that which remaineth boiled in the bottome, which they laie up and keepe untill occasion serveth to use it. They put hereunto Eleeoselinum, Aconitum, Frondes populeas and Soote.

Rx. Sium, acarum vulgare, pentaphyllon, the blood of a flitter mouse, solanum somniferum and oleum. They stampe all these togither, and then they rubbe all parts of their bodys exceedinglie till they look red and be verie hot, so as the pores may be opened and their flesh soluble and loose. They joine herewithall either fat, or oil in steed thereof, that the force of the ointment maie the rather pearse inwardly and so be more effectuall. By this means in a moonlight night they seeme to be carried in the aire to feasting, singing, dansing, kissing, culling and other acts of venerie with such youthes as they love and desire most. For the force . . . of their imagination is so vehement that almost all that part of the braine wherein the memorie consisteth is full of such conceipts.

—*Discoverie of Witchcraft,* X. viii

9. A Gentlewoman at Lyons

There was (saith M. Bodin) a noble Gentlewoman at Lions, that being in bed with a lover of hirs, suddenlie in the night arose up and lighted a candle, which when she had done, she took a box of ointment, wherewith she annointed her bodie, and after a few words spoken she was carried awaie. Her bedfellow, seeing the order thereof, lept out of his bed, tooke the candle in his hand, and sought for the ladie round about the chamber and in everie corner thereof. But though he could not find hir, yet did he find hir box of ointment. And being desirous to know the vertue thereof, besmeered himself therewith, even as he perceived hir to have done. And although he were not so superstitious as to use anie words to helpe him forward in his busines, yet by the vertue of that ointment (saith Bodin) he was immediatelie conveied to Lorreine into the assemblie of witches. Which when he saw he was abashed, and said, "In the name of God, what make I here?" And upon these words the whole assemblie vanished awaie, and left him there alone starke naked, and so he was faine to returne to Lions. But he had so good a conscience (for you may perceive by the first part of the historie he was a verie honest man) that he accused his true lover for a witch and caused hir to be burned.

—*Discoverie of Witchcraft*, III. v

10. The Devil's Dinners

All those who have eaten at the devil's table state that his dinners are both so disgusting to look at or stink so that the hungriest diner feels sick. Sybilla Morele stated that there was every sort of food set before them, but so badly cooked that it could hardly be swallowed. Nicolas Morele said it tasted so bitter that he had to spit it out, and that when the devil saw him do this he became furious. As for the drink, it was like clots of dark blood in a dirty cup.

—*Demonolatry*, I. xvi

11. A Succubus at Hemingen

Melchior Eric, a very reliable fellow, reported that there was a witch brought to trial at Hemingen, and that the judge asked him how he had first been induced to commit such foul deeds, in a word, how it had come about that the devil seduced him.

He replied that he had been in charge of the cattle, and that one morning, going to round them up, he had caught sight of the young girl whose task it was to open the barn doors. At the very first glimpse of her she had roused in him so sudden and so strong a passion that he could think of nothing else, night or day. One afternoon, being alone in a meadow and thinking of her as usual, suddenly he had caught sight of her (or what he thought to be her) hiding behind a bush. He had been quite overcome with desire, and so of course he had run up and taken hold of her. She had struggled, but having once got his hands on her he simply could not let go. So at last, after a good deal of pleading on his part, she gave in, but only on two conditions. He had to swear that he would openly acknowledge her as his mistress, and he had to promise that he would treat her as if she were a goddess.

This he agreed to do, and so he had his will of her. But as soon as he was finished it seemed as though she herself were overpowered by lust, and he was forced to satisfy her again and again, so that from then on he found himself in the miserable position of being perpetually at the beck and call of her desires.

We ought here to mention the succubus Abrahel, of Petronius Armentarius in Dalheim. No doubt she was overcome by jealousy at the thought that he might love anyone but her. In any case, she actually induced him to prove his love by murdering his only son. When he had done the deed and gone nearly out of his mind with remorse, she told him that if he only kept adoring her enough she would be able to bring the boy back to life. And so it came to pass. For a whole year by means of her magic spells she made it look as though the child were actually living in the house. But of course it was no more than a trick, for when suddenly the boy died for the second time his body began all at once to stink so frightfully that even the father found it quite impossible to go anywhere near it.

Philostratus tells us in his life of Apollonius of Tyana that the same thing happened to Menippus, a disciple of the cynic, Demetrius. He was on the road from Corinth to Cenchreae when he met what looked to be a rich and ravishingly beautiful foreign girl who announced not only that she had fallen in love with him, but that she wanted him to go home with her at once. He, too, felt an overpowering passion, and the result was that he lay with her night after night. They even began to talk about marriage. Her house was positively regal. But Apollonius examined the place very carefully and warned the young man that she was a Lamia. If he did not free himself at once she would end by devouring him, or at least by doing him very serious harm.

—*Demonolatry*, II. i

12. How the Devil Marries Young Women

Colette Fischer, tried in Mainz in May, 1585 (and many other witches too) stated that it was very common for the devil to marry one of his followers. Betrande Barbier and Sinchen May, tried at Forbach in August, 1587, said that they had often been present at such weddings when these happened to be celebrated at night at some spot where criminals had been executed. Instead of giving the girl a ring, the devil would bend down and blow into her arsehole.

—*Demonolatry*, II. ii

13. The Use of Dead Bodies to Make Magic

Our modern witches even put dead bodies to use, particularly if they can lay hands on the corpse of an executed felon. Not only do they use bits of the cadavers to make charms. They use the devices that were employed in the execution too, the rope or chains, the stake or the manacles. They believe there is a virtue in such things.

Indeed, what other purpose can they have in acquiring the corpses of aborted babies? Of their skin they make a kind of parchment on which they write uncouth words intended to bring about the fulfillment of their desires. Agrippa, Petrus de Abano and Weyer, all past masters in diabolic magic, have set down notes on these matters that are quite beyond belief.

Sometimes they cook the foetus entire until it is either turned to ashes or melted into a fatty glue with which they can mix other ingredients. Giovanni Batista Porta states in his *Natural Magic, Book II* that such concoctions were brewed even in his day, and Pliny informs us that not only midwives, but even certain whores were accustomed to dismember abortions in order to brew poisons for their crimes. The same is done today in German Lorraine. I have found it to be a fact during my own examinations of witches brought before me for their capital offences.

At Dieuze in October, 1586, Anna Ruffa admitted that with a witch called Lolla she had dug up a body lately buried at Dieuze Gate, and that from its ashes they had compounded a poison certain to kill anyone who swallowed it. Catherine of Metingow confessed in September, 1586, that to make a poison more unpleasant she had generally added lupine, fern, unula campana, ox gall, soot, or anything else she could find that was bitter, for no matter how hard the victim struggled they simple stuffed the poison down his throat.

Meg Bricq of Forbach (testimony of August, 1587) gave similar evidence, for she told us about digging up the corpse of a child that had been buried by its father, Faber Wolf, the previous day. In only one point did Wolf's evidence differ from that of the women, for he told us that he did not incinerate the body, but melted it into a glutinous mass out of which he was able to prepare an ointment more easily. Later he burned the bones to ashes. With these he sprinkled fruit trees so that the crop might fail.

Fuxena Eugel of Buligny (April, 1586) reported likewise that she used to scatter ashes into the wind, using charms and curses at the same time to burn out blossoms or poison crops.

Johann Schneider's wife, Maria, of Metzereth, reported to us that a premature child was born to Joanette Mathes, and that the woman buried it secretly under the earthen floor of her house. But several witches heard about this, dug the body up and boiled it to make an ointment. Maria Schneider herself rubbed the ointment onto the handle of a broom, and when she put it between her legs it carried her through the air to Bruch, where her diabolical master, one Rousgen, had decided to hold a Sabbat.

Antoine Welsch of Guermingen reported in December, 1589, that female witches in Gross Michel and Besskess did similar things. They dug up two bodies in Guermingen cemetery that had been buried by parents recently bereaved. After burning the dead children, they had used the bodies for their magical purposes. First of all they had cut off the right arms with shoulders and ribs attached. These were to be used as lights in case they wanted to poison anyone at night. A marvelous business, and one might suppose it to be a mere figment of the imagination. They reported, however, that the dead fingertips would burn with a blue flame until they had finished whatever they were about, but that when the flames were put out the fingers would be found as clean and uninjured as though they had never been used. This turned out to be true no matter how often it was tried. Not long after Welsch told me this story, the wife of one Bernhardi told me a similar one in Guermingen (January, 1590). She readily admitted a horrid crime against her own child. For purely diabolical purposes she had pulled it to pieces, roasted it and then destroyed the bits that were left.

—*Demonolatry*, II. iii

* * *

For a variety of reasons the murder of children for occult reasons was not confined to practitioners of European witchcraft. Here are two not dissimilar stories from Africa.

14. A Child Sacrificed in Africa

At Likwanga there was a child who had cut its upper teeth before the lower ones. Its father, doing what he could to rescue it from the awful destiny that normally befell such children, had kept it hidden for eight whole years. But an enemy told Kalonga the truth of the matter, arguing that all the deaths and misfortunes in the village were the fault of this child. . . . When the father came to me I told him to bring us the child as soon as he could. But a few days later he returned and told me that they had strangled his son and thrown him into the lake.

—A. AND E. JALA, *Pionniers parmi les marotse*

15. Obligatory Death of a Child in Africa

I was the oldest boy in our family, and I had a smaller sister. One day the priest (the medicine man) turned up at our house. First he glanced at my father, then at my sister, and then he said, "You realize that your daughter is going to die."

"Why?" my father asked.

"Before she was born," the priest told him, "you hunted pigs. You killed snakes. You carried loads on your back. And because of these things you are going to lose your daughter. Why bother to feed her? There is nothing you can do that will make any difference. She is going to die."

So at his wits' end, my father went to my mother and told her what had happened. They were both quite distracted. But what could they do?

At last my father came to a decision. "We have to kill the girl," he said. "What is the use of letting her eat our rice?"

And I was a big fellow by then, so he made me fetch a sack, stuff my sister into it and take her out into the forest.

—*Berichte der rheinischen Missionsgesellschaft*, 1909

* * *

For a slight variation on the theme, see Anthropos, *v. p.* 946.

16. Eating Salt During Pregnancy

Women (in Uganda) may not eat salt during their pregnancy. If they do so, it is believed that the child will die. When therefore a newborn child falls ill, the husband blames his wife for the fact, saying, "This child is dying of an illness caused by your having eaten salt."

17. Unbaptized Infants Dug Up in Scotland

Helen Guthrie and four companions dug up the body of an unbaptized infant in 1661 and took severall peices thereof, as the feet, hands, a pairt of the head and a pairt of the buttocks, and they made a py thereof, that they might eat of it, that by this meanes they might never make a confession (as they thought) of their witchcraftis.

—George Ritchie Kinloch,
Religiae Antiquiae Scoticae, Edinburgh, 1848

18. Mme. de Montespan's Mass

Mlle. Montvoison, aged eighteen, had presented at Mme. de Montespan's mass (and at her mother's order) an infant born before term. She had placed it in a bowl. (Abbe) Guibourg had slaughtered it and consecrated its blood with the host . . . *Guibourg bought another* child to be sacrificed at this mass for one ecu. It had been sold him by a girl. Having first drawn its blood, he cut its throat with a knife and poured the blood into a chalice. Then the body was taken off to another place and its heart and entrails brought back to him so that he might make another sacrifice.

—François Ravaisson, *Archives de la Bastille,* Paris, 1873

The justices of the peace were seen familiarly conversing with the foul fiend, to whom one in Dumfries-shire actually offered up his firstborn child immediately after birth, stepping out with it in his arms to the staircase, where the devil stood ready, as it was suspected, to receive the innocent victim.

—C. K. Sharpe, *Historical Account of Witchcraft in Scotland,* London, 1884

He teacheth them to make ointments of the bowels and members of children, whereby they ride in the aire, and accomplish all their desires. So as if there be anie children unbaptised or not garded with the signe of the crosse or [with] orizons, then the witches may and doe catch them from their mothers sides in the night, or out of their cradles, or otherwise kill them with their ceremonies, and after buriall steele them out of their graves and seeth them in a caldron untill their flesh be made potable. Of the thickest whereof they make ointments whereby they ride in the aire. But the thinner portion they put into flaggons, whereof whosoever drinketh, observing certain ceremonies, immediatelie becommeth a maister or rather a mistress in that practise and facultie.

—*Discoverie of Witchcraft*

19. Killing Children to Cause Dissension

Catherine Ruffa confessed at Ville sur Moselle in June, 1587, that she had often slipped into people's houses at night down the chimney and turned babies face down on their pillows to smother them. But she always managed to leave a clue that would make the husband blame his wife for what had happened. And so she would not only kill the child but start the couple quarrelling, and this the devil loves, to cause dissension among lovers.

Alexée Belheure (the case was heard at Blainville in January, 1587) was constantly at loggerheads with her husband, and of course this is generally the case in poverty stricken households where they lack even the simplest necessities. But Alexée's loathing reached such a pitch that it was only her inability to attack the man successfully, not her good nature, that restrained her. In the end the devil came to her help, for he offered to attack the man in her place if she wished. So she dropped to her knees in front of him, and in the end he told her he would do what he could.

Now it so happened that on Christmas Eve the poor fellow went to a nearby town to buy a few of the little gifts and decorations that happy households generally enjoy at that time of year. But late that night as he was on his way home the devil caught him, beat him unmercifully and threw him into the ravine at Donalibaria. Then hurrying back to the wife he told her what he had done.

—*Demonolatry*, II. vii

20. A Witch Turns into a Dog

One year when the peasants brought their loads of fuel up to the Signiory at Pettelengo to exchange them for food, their dogs began fighting in the castle hall, and one old bitch ran and hid in a stove that was sometimes used for heating water. The rest of the rabble began barking more fiercely than ever, so one of the servants peered into the oven to see what was amiss, and finding the bitch cowering there, a more hideous creature than all the rest, slashed at it with his knife and gave it a fearful wound in the muzzle. At this the bitch rushed howling out into the yard and disappeared.

A little while afterward there began to be talk all over the town of an old hag lying in her bed, wounded, without being able to tell who had done it to her. At once people began to put two and two together, and they realized that she was the old bitch wounded at the hall. So of course, because of this and because of her vile reputation, she was arrested and locked up in prison. After she had been carefully questioned she at last confessed the truth of what everyone suspected, and admitted many other acts of witchcraft as well.

—*Demonolatry*, II. iv

* * *

All those confessions so readily made and written down, the details not hitherto suspected, the falling over oneself to incriminate oneself as deeply as possible. It passes the bounds of credulity. For as the prisoner knew only too well, the epilogue to confession (at least in France and Germany) was a slow and terrible death at the stake. But inquisitors had ways of opening stubborn mouths, and although verbatim accounts of the procedure are not common, there exists one account that makes the method of interrogation very plain. For prisoners were not broken down by adroit questioning or by piling up evidence against them until confession became the only rational reply. No, one simply hammered away with simple accusations repeated over and over again until the desired admission came. But that was not enough, for then followed a demand for the names of accomplices, and sometimes these had to be invented. Then words, acts, scenes, details had to be invented too until the entire story the inquisitor wanted to hear had taken shape. Very few indeed, once they had been put to the question, ever escaped. The following account of the interrogation of one Dominic Gordel, a simple parish priest accused of witchcraft, is taken from the Notes pour servir à l'histoire du chapitre de Saint-Die *of François de Chanteau. It appears in slightly different form in Robbins'* Encyclopedia of Witchcraft and Demonology, New York, 1959. *It is not for the squeamish.*

21. The Torture of Father Dominic Gordel

La Joliette Tower in the Palace of Toul. The examination began at one o'clock on the afternoon of the 26th of April, 1631. There were present M. Jean Midot, Archdeacon and Canon of Toul, M. Antoine d'Antan, priest of the Lord of Sitie, M. Charles Mathiot, Doctor of Medicine and M. Jean Marson, surgeon, of Toul. These latter had been asked to witness that no unnecessary violence was used on the prisoner.

We first warned the said prisoner, Gordel, how serious the charges were that had been laid against him, and advised him as strongly as we were able that it would be better for him to confess his crimes than force us to employ the tortures that had been got ready. We caused him to swear on the Holy Gospels (placing his hands on the book) that he would speak nothing but the truth. He stated that he was not a sorcerer, and that he had never made a pact of any kind with the devil.

Upon this we ordered M. Poirson, Executioner of the city of Toul, to affix thumbscrews to those fingers of the left hand not used in making the benediction. As soon as the screws were tightened the accused cried out upon Jesus and Mary, and repeated that he had never been a sorcerer. So the machine was fixed to the identical fingers of his right hand. Upon this, he cried out simply, "St. Nicholas!"

Asked if he had made a pact with the Devil, he replied that he had not and wished only to die in God's arms. So we ordered the screws to be applied to his toes. Again he affirmed that he had never been to a Sabbat. "Jesus and Mary!" he cried, and a moment later, "Mary, mother of God! Blessed Jesus!"

Asked if he had taken Claude Cathelinotte to the Sabbat, he answered, "No. I have never been to a Sabbat."

So we ordered him to be placed on the ladder and stretched. The straps were tightened to pull him to the first rung, and once again he was asked if he had been to a Sabbat and there made a pact with the Devil. To this he said, "Jesus! Mary! I am dying." Again it was demanded of him if he had ever been a sorcerer, or had married any couples at a Sabbat. He said, "No!" It was duly noted that up to this point in his questioning, the only words he had spoken were *Jesus* and *Mary,* and that he had denied ever making a pact with the Devil or attending a Sabbat.

We ordered him to be released for a moment, and then again stretched on the ladder. He kept crying out, "Jesus! Mary! St. Nicholas! Mother of God, help me." He was asked if he had attended a Sabbat, and he answered, "No!" Thereupon he was stretched a little further, and he called out, "Jesus, I am dying."

Once more he was warned to speak nothing but the truth. If he did so, he would be released. But still he maintained that he had not been to a Sabbat, and said, "Mother of God, help me." He was admonished that it would be best if he renounced any pacts that he had made with the Devil. To this he answered that he renounced them all, and that he had not been to a Sabbat. He was asked how many times he had attended the devilish gathering and whom he had seen there. His answer was that he had seen no one, that he did not even know what a Sabbat was. Then he cried out again, "St. Nicholas! Blessed Jesus. God have mercy upon me! They are tearing an innocent man's body."

Once again we ordered that his bonds be loosened a moment. Then for the third time he was stretched onto the ladder and advised that it would be easier for him if he told the truth. But again, all he would say was, "I am dying. St. Nicholas! Jesus and Mary! I am being murdered. Blessed Mary, do not abandon me."

Asked about an occasion when he had cured a person whose eye had come out of its socket, he replied that he had used nothing except olive oil and the name of God. This entire time he kept calling on Jesus, Mary and St. Nicholas, asking them not to abandon him, and praying that his soul be in God's arms. "I have never witnessed a Sabbat," he cried out. "I have made no images. I have no magical powders." Then in Latin he called out, *"Libera me a calumniis hominum. Maria mater gratiae, mater misericordiae."* Then he called upon St. Dominic. *"Mater. Mater gratiae,"* he cried. *"Mater misericordiae, tu nos ob hoste protege et hora mortis suscipe."*

He was admonished not to put such great faith in the Devil, who was a deceiver, but he only repeated that he had never made a pact with the Devil.

So we ordered the thongs to be loosened again, and all the while he kept crying out, "I am dying. I can bear it no longer." Again and again he was adjured to remember his soul's salvation, for in the light of so many accusations pointing him out, his guilt was established beyond any question. He was asked to take pity on his own body. He had exorcised Devils improperly, so he must on the face of it be guilty either of witchcraft or heresy.

He answered that if he had ever performed an improper exorcism he hoped he would be pardoned, but he had never been a sorcerer.

So there being no other course we could take, we had the screws fixed to his left side, to arm, thigh and calf. But with utter stubbornness he kept crying out that he had never been to a Sabbat. "I am dying," he added. "They are crushing me. Jesus! Mary! I renounce Satan."

It was ordered that the screws be tightened, but he only kept shouting that he was telling the truth. He had never been to a Sabbat. And continually he kept repeating, "Jesus! Mary! Father in heaven, help me. Mother of God, have mercy. No compact with the Devil. I have never let myself be tempted."

Still the screws were tightened, and he positively screamed out, "Jesus! Mary! Father in heaven, help me. It is crushing me. I never saw a Sabbat. I never was at a Sabbat. I renounce the Devil. I believe in the Holy Trinity. I place myself in the hands of the blessed angels. Pity! I pray God for pity."

So at last we commanded that he be taken down from the ladder (where he had been stretched for about a quarter of an hour) and carried over to the fire. We warned him that he must bear the divine judgement in mind, for it could not be evaded. He might escape the judgement of his fellow mortals, but in the end, if he had any care for his soul, he must speak the truth.

He only said that he had always tried to be a good man and a good priest, that he had committed none of the crimes of which he had been accused. So we left him beside his fire in the Tower of La Joliette with a guard assigned to keep watch, and he signed this record of the procedings on the day and year above named.

Signed: J. Midot; C. Mathiot; J. Marson.
  C. de Gournay, Bishop of Sitie and Vicar-General.
  Dom Husson, Secretary.

* * *

Francesco Maria Guazzo died about 1640. The date of his birth—and almost everything else about him—is unknown. But that he was a contemplative, a gentle and highly learned man is perfectly clear from all he wrote. Here is no urbane and righteous burner of witches like Remy. Guazzo is not even a purely rational raconteur like Reginald Scot. No, in this good priest we meet a Brother of the Ambrosian Order, a creature utterly innocent, utterly wide-eyed, and credulous. He accepts it as a fact that Luther was fathered by the devil on a nun, and in Book II of his great work he notes it as another simple fact that when Luther died the demons flew to his funeral out of the mouths of many who had been possessed. But he is not to be tricked. When a cow in Belgium gives birth to a normal child, he suggests that the story is very likely an imposture. So his Compendium Maleficarum *is an amalgam of faith, innocence, and an almost encyclopedic knowledge of the learned authorities. If his stories are not true, he makes one wish they were. For in a time like Guazzo's, cruel, corrupt and ignorant, a time when indeed the people in many a sullen hamlet openly worshiped the devil as part of their rebellion against clerical authority, Guazzo simply worked away year after year at the many books in his Milanese library. They say that when the learned Pope Nicholas V visited Fabriano, the city stank for three days of burning flesh. Whether Milan stank so we do not know. But if it had, Guazzo would probably not even have noticed. He would have been walking, one imagines, in some garden's dappled sunlight, smiling perhaps, because of his quiet certainty that, like him, God was both innocent and good.*

22. A Girl Discovers Her Mother's Witchcraft

There was a young and innocent girl who lived in Bergamo with her mother. But one night, to everyone's horror and astonishment, they found her naked in the bed of her brother-in-law in Venice almost sixty leagues away. Of course they recognized her at once, found her some clothes and asked what she was doing there.

And in floods of tears she told them. "It was the middle of the night and I was awake," she said. "But my mother thought I slept. I saw her rise, slip out of her shift and rub her body with ointment out of a pot she had hidden in a cubicle. Then she climbed a stick as though it were a horse, and it lifted her off the floor and straight out of the window.

"I could not make out where she had gone. So I got out of bed too and rubbed the same stuff on my body, and at once I was carried out through the window and flew through the air until suddenly I found myself here. My mother was standing beside my brother-in-law's bed, and she seemed to be threatening him. It frightened me, and my sudden arrival seemed to frighten her too. I called on Jesus and Mary, at which suddenly my mother vanished, and I found myself here, naked and alone."

So the girl's brother-in-law wrote down what she had said and carried this testimony to the Inquisitor General at Bergamo. He had the mother arrested. She was put to the torture and confessed everything, saying that the devil had taken her to the boy's room fifty times and more, but that she had never been able to kill him because his parents had protected him so well with the crucifix and holy prayers.

—*Compendium Maleficarum*, I. xii

23. A Scottish Incubus

I have read of a gently born young woman who lived on the shores of the Moray Firth in Scotland, an exceptionally beautiful girl who turned down any number of young men in marriage because she had begun indulging in certain filthy practices with an incubus. When her horrified parents heard about this, they of course demanded not only that she confess the full extent of her depravity, but—what was more important—that she tell them the name of her lover.

At last, desperate and cornered with their questions, she admitted that she had met a wonderfully handsome young man who crept into her bedroom at night and lay with her. Sometimes they did this even by day, but where he came from, or where he went when he left her she did not know.

Of course they found this difficult to believe, so they decided to lie in wait and find out just who it was that had so cruelly deprived their daughter of her virginity. And sure enough, three nights later a maidservant came running to tell them that the girl's lover was actually in the house. Without any more ado they bolted the doors, collected torches and broke into her room. There, naked in the girl's arms, they beheld a monster uglier than any they had ever imagined.

By this time others had arrived, among them a holy father learned in exorcism, and while the family turned their backs or ran out of the room in horror, he began in a clear voice to intone the Gospel according to St. John. When he came to "The word was made flesh," the incubus shrieked out in terror, set fire to the bed and flew off, taking the roof with him on his way.

A little while afterward the girl gave birth to an infant of unbelievable loathsomeness, and to prevent its being seen and bringing disgrace on the family, the midwives burned it.

—*Compendium Maleficarum*, I. xi

24. Another Scot's Succubus Defeated

About fourteen miles from Aberdeen there was a very handsome young man who went to his bishop and complained that he was troubled by a succubus, a creature more lissome and lovely than any woman he had ever met. She came to him at night, he said, even when he had locked the doors, crept into bed with him, wheedled him into embracing her, and stayed until daybreak, scarcely ever making so much as a sound. Over and over again he had tried to free himself from this disgusting relationship, but always in vain.

The good bishop ordered him to move house and set his mind to thoughts of the Christian faith—to fast and pray. And lo and behold, when he acted on the venerable man's advice, in a few days the young gentleman found himself delivered.

—*Compendium Maleficarum*, I. xii

25. A Husband Falls in Love with a Witch

There was a young husband in San Geminiano who fell so deeply in love with a witch that he left wife and children to live with her. But his wife, certain that he had simply been put under a spell, hunted everywhere for the magic that had induced it. And sure enough, under her own bed she found a jar wherein somebody had stuffed a toad with its eyes sewn shut. She pulled it out, cut the stitches to open its eyes, then burned it. At once her husband returned to her as though his love affair with the witch had been nothing but a dream.
—*Compendium Maleficarum*, II. iv

* * *

Reginald Scot had no patience with stories of incubi and succubi, or with the prurient and voyeurist interest in sex that characterized so many witch-finders and inquisitors. He ridicules them not only by carrying them to extremes, but by adding that some of the female saints would have been all the better if they could have found a lusty young incubus between their legs.

26. Reginald Scot Ridicules the Incubus

You shall read in the legend how in the night time Incubus came to a ladies bed side and made hot loove unto hir; whereat she being offended, cried out so lowd that companie came and found him under hir bed in the likeness of the holie bishop Sylvanus, which holie man was much defamed thereby, untill at the length this infamie was purged by the confession of a divell made at S. Jerome's toombe.

Oh, excellent peece of witchcraft or cousening wrought by

Sylvanus! *Item:* S. Christine would needes take unto hir another maides Incubus and lie in hir roome: and the storie saith that she was shrewdly accloied.* But she was a shrew indeed that would needes change beds with hir fellow that was troubled everie night with Incubus and deale with him hir selfe.

But here the inquisitors note maie not be forgotten, to wit, that Maides having yellow haire are most molested with this spirit. Also it is written in the Legend of S. Barnard that a pretie wench that had had the use of Incubus his bodie by the space of six or seven yeares in Aquitania (being beelike wearie of him for that he waxed old) would needes go to S. Barnard another while. But Incubus told hir that if she would so forsake him (being so loong hir true loover), he would be revenged on hir, &c. But befall what would, she went to S. Barnard who tooke hir his staffe and bad hir laie it in the bed beside hir. And indeed, the divell fearing the bedstaffe, or that S. Barnard laie there himselfe, durst not approach into hir chamber that night. What he did afterwards I am uncerteine. Marrie you may find other circumstances hereof, and many other like bawdie lies in the golden Legend. But here againe we maie not forget the inquisitors note, to wit, that manie are so bewitched that they cannot use their own wives, but anie other bodies they may well enough away withall. Which witchcraft is practiced among manie bad husbands, for whom it were a good excuse to saie they were bewitched.

—*Discoverie of Witchcraft,* IV. v

* * *

It is quite apparent that Guazzo took the material for the next excerpt from Remy's Demonolatry. *His very style is changed by Remy's more acute understanding of sex in its practical aspects.*

---

*To accloy is to drive in a nail. Thus to be accloyed is to have something like a nail driven into one.

27. How Children Are Infected with Witchcraft

The disease of witchcraft often spreads like any other infection from parent to child, especially when the mother has been trying to ingratiate herself with the devil. For Satan's greed is endless and insatiable. Once let him get a foothold in any house, and it is very hard indeed to drive him out. It is an almost certain proof against one accused of witchcraft if a parent has already been condemned. And we hear daily of cases where the crime has been inherited, for the devil is industrious in adding to the numbers of his followers. What better way of achieving that end than by inducing those followers to corrupt their children?

In October, 1568, at Girancourt, one Domenico Petronius reported that before he was twelve years old his mother had taken him to diabolical meetings to find him a wife.

In January, 1587, Nicolle Morelle confessed in Barr that her father had taken her to meetings with the devil before she had even reached the age of puberty. Another girl, still physically a child, was taken into a thick forest by her mother, and told that she would meet a young man there whom she might possibly marry. Just as her mother had promised, he appeared, but as soon as she lay down with him she sensed something amiss, for his weight on her was as heavy and unbending as marble.

In July, 1568, a certain Henry and Catherine, a couple who lived in Gebweiler, found a succubus for their son, Hans. All he could tell when he first laid eyes on her was that her dress and her hair were black, and that her feet looked like horses' hooves. But nevertheless he felt a huge hunger to possess her, and being emptied of all holy thoughts, seized her with greedy lust. But as soon as he had entered her body he felt as though his member had gone into some icy cave. So he desisted and went away very sad and ashamed.

In the neighbourhood of Ribeauville a certain Dominique Falvet was with her mother one day, cutting rushes to tie up the vines. After a while they both lay down to rest. And as they talked, the mother remarked casually that if anything unusual happened she must not be afraid, for nothing would

harm her. Suddenly there appeared a man who looked like a shoemaker, for he had lengths of pitch-soaked twine wrapped round his waist. The girl was made to swear allegiance to this fellow, and in token that she had done so he scratched her on the forehead with one of his fingernails. Then in front of her mother's very eyes he stretched her on the ground and copulated with her. When he had finished he did the same to the mother while the girl sat and watched. After this they all took hands and danced in a ring for a little while. Then he gave them what looked like money, but later it turned to dust in their hands and finally vanished into thin air, and the man went back to wherever he had come from.
—*Compendium Maleficarum*, II. iv

28. A Girl Betrays Her Mother as a Witch

A little girle walking abroad with hir father in his land heard him complaine of drought, wishing for raine, &c. Whie father (quoth the child) I can make it raine or haile when and where I list. He asked where she learned it. She said of hir mother, who forbad hir to tell anie bodie thereof. He asked hir how hir mother taught hir. She answered that hir mother committed hir to a maister who would at anie time doo anie thing for hir. Whie then (said he), make it raine, but only in my field. And so she went to the streame and threw up water in hir maisters name, and made it raine presentlie. And proceeding further with her father, she made it haile in another field at hir father's request. Hereupon he accused his wife and caused hir to be burned. And then he new christened his child againe: which circumstance is common among papists and witchmongers.
—*Discoverie of Witchcraft*, III. xiii

* * *

Unlike Remy, who writes down what he has seen or been told, Guazzo sets down the fruit of his voluminous reading.

29. Midwives and Whores Who Murder Children

Sprenger tells the story of two midwives who were burned alive, one in Bale and one in Strasbourg. The first had murdered forty and the other an uncomputed number of new-born infants by thrusting needles into their heads.

Xiphilinus and Dio Cassius write that at the time of the Emperor Domitian many people were arrested for pricking victims with poisoned pins so that they died without even feeling any pain. The same thing happened during the reign of the Emperor Commodus.

Johann Nider says that in the Berne district there were witches of both sexes who murdered and ate their own children. Others committed the same crimes near Lausanne.

A certain lawyer from Frankfurt reports that a few years ago eight witches were burned there for murdering a total of a hundred and forty children. And in the year 1553 two female witches in Berlin were caught in the act of trying to bring down a fruit-killing frost. They had kidnapped a neighbour's child, then cut up the body and cooked it. But by God's will the mother came upon them and caught sight of the pot with her little one's arms and legs sticking out. So of course the malefactors were arrested and put to the torture. They confessed that if they had managed to finish cooking the broth there would have been a terrible frost, and all the fruit round about would have been destroyed.

—*Compendium Maleficarum*, II. iii

30. Sorcerers in India

I was told by two men [in India] that they believed that a sorcerer, by merely thinking of the effect he wished to produce, could produce the effect, and that it was not necessary for him to use any magical formula or practice any special rites.

—W. H. R. RIVERS, *The Todas*

When rain is wanted if anyone runs out of the house bare-headed while it is raining, he is ordered in at once, or he is told to put on his cap or turban, for a bareheaded man is apt to wish involuntarily that the rain might cease, and thus injure his neighbour.

—W. CROOKE, *The Popular Religion and Folk-lore of Northern India,* I (1896)

31. Sickness and Death in the Congo

Sickness and death are considered by a Congo to be quite abnormal; they are in no way to be traced to natural causes, but always regarded as due to sorcery. Even such cases as death by drowning or in war, by a fall from a tree, or by some beast of prey or wild creature, or by lightning—these are all in a most obstinate and unreasoning manner attributed to the black art. Somebody has bewitched the sufferer, and he or she who caused it is a witch.

—W. H. BENTLEY, *Pioneering in the Congo,* 1900

32. Trial of the *Elamango*

Every native who possesses a *mango* is an *elamango*. Any deformity in an organ, any deformity of the stomach is a particular sign that the *mango* is there. So that natives use the word for the belly and rennet bag of a ruminant's stomach. According to them the *mango* is generally near the stomach, at the top of the intestine. It is a fleshy protuberance. Some people have two of them. The *mango* enables the one who has it to possess the power of witchcraft. The *elamango* is thus a wizard. According to the Azandi he possesses supernatural powers, can cast lots, cause a death, bring about accidents . . . Such a man can see no matter how dark the night; he can slip into a kraal without a sound and cause people there to fall into a deep sleep. He can also take away the witchcraft and cure a man whose death he has wished for, and to make him use this power, the *elamango* are told that they will be killed if one of their victims dies . . .

Whoever is thought to be an *elamango* must submit to trial by *benget*, which is a poison from the root of a tree. *Benget* is the oracle . . . and can find out the invisible *mango* in the *elamango's* body and overcome it. First the *benget* is tried out on a chicken or a dog, and the animal dies. Then the accused must drink, and very often his accuser is required to do the same. The one who dies is guilty. If it is the accused, he was a witch. If it is the accuser, he was a slanderer . . . But even so, the death of the accused is not enough. A post-mortem must show the *mango* in his belly. If it is not found, the accuser is forced to pay an indemnity to the relatives, a female slave and a certain number of spears . . .

But sometimes a native accused of having the *mango* in him does not have to undergo the ordeal himself. His son may take his place, or if it is a woman, her daughter, for the *mango* is inherited by sons from fathers and by daughters from mothers. Sometimes, indeed, the man accused of being *elamango* does not wait to undergo the ordeal. He kills one of his children, trusting the post-mortem to prove his innocence.

—HUTEREAU, *Notes sur la vie familiale et juridique de quelques population du Congo belge. (Annales du Musée du Congo belge. Documents ethnographiques, series I.)*

33. The Doomed Heretic of Cambrai

There was an extremely clever heretic in the neighbourhood of Cambrai, and he lived in perpetual terror of being burned alive by the friars, who at that time were putting a good many to the stake. So he pretended to have a demon in him, and his friends tied him hand and foot and carried him to the shrine of St. Aichard at Dour, for St. Aichard has power to cast out devils. The point was that they thought him mad and not heretical.

But a cleric was also there, tied up like the heretic because he really was possessed by the devil. And when he heard that Eloi Bougris (that was the heretic's name) was in the place, by God's will he broke his thongs and, rushing in to where the heretic lay, piled straw, benches, mats, whatever he could find in the church on top of the fellow. Eloi took it for a joke until the cleric caught up a burning lamp and tried to set the pile on fire. Seeing this, he screamed for help, and the gaolers came running to put the fire out. But the cleric, taking up a sword, drove them all back so that the heretic was burned alive. And as soon as he saw the heretic dead he was himself cured, and the devil left him.

—THOMAS OF BRABANT, *Bonum Universale, Book II*

* * *

One of the charges leveled on witches by Innocent VIII was that they caused impotence in men and barrenness in women. The following story from Guazzo and two excerpts from Reginald Scot are examples of credulity and mockery in dealing with the charge.

34. The Adulterous Porter of Bassompierre

There was an old man, a porter at the Chateau de Bassompierre, who married a young wife while he was still living in adultery with a mistress. And of course his wife felt wretched at the thought of having to share him with a strumpet not half as young and pretty as she. So, as women usually do, she talked about it to a neighbour and asked what she ought to do.

Her neighbour, a woman called Laire, advised her to take

courage, for she knew a cure for such troubles. She picked a plant out of her garden and gave it to her. If she made a broth out of that plant, the wife was told, and gave it to her husband to drink, he would quite forget the old mistress.

So on the very next day the broth was served at dinner, and at once the husband fell into a deep sleep. When he awoke next morning he found to his horror that he was no longer able to have an erection, and as he could not hope to hide the fact from his wife, he told her what had happened to him.

She, realizing at once that her neighbour had betrayed her, and that by trying to keep the man entirely to herself she had lost him, confessed what she had done. Since he had to acknowledge that he had only his own lechery to blame, he forgave her at once and went to his lord, François de Bassompierre, to ask what ought to be done.

That nobleman, anxious both to help his servant and to punish the witch for her wickedness, had the woman sent for and threatened her with such dire punishment that at last she restored the man's virility by giving him a second plant to eat. This demonstrated her guilt beyond any question, so she was arrested and burned at the stake.

—*Compendium Maleficarum*, II. vii

35. Witches Attack Men's Masculinity

A young priest at Mespurge in the diocese of Constance was bewitched so as he had no power to occupie any other or mo women than one, and to be delivered out of that thraldome, sought to flie into another countrie where he might use that preestlie occupation more freelie. But all in vaine, for evermore he was brought as far backward by night as he went forward in the daie before, sometimes by land, sometimes in the aire, as though he flew. And if this be not true, I am sure that James Sprenger doth lie.

For the further confirmation of our beleefe in Incubus, *Malleus Maleficarum* citeth a storie of a notable matter executed at Ravenspurge, as true and as cleanlie as the rest. A young man lieng with a wench in that towne (saith he) was faine to leave his instruments of venerie behind him by means of that prestigious art of witchcraft, so as in that place nothing could be seene or felt but his plaine bodie. This yoong man was willed by another witch to go to hir that he suspected, and by faire or fowle means to require hir helpe, who soone after meeting with hir, intreated hir faire, but that was in vaine, and therefore he caught hir by the throte, and with a towell strangled hir, saieng, Restore me my toole or thou shalt die for it. So as she being swolne and blacke in the face and through his boisterous handling ready to die, said, Let me go and I will helpe thee. And whilest he was loosing the towell she put hir hand into his codpeece and touched the place, saieng, Now hast thou thy desire, and even at that instant he felt himself restored.

Item, a reverend father, for his life, holiness and knowledge notorious, being a frier of the order and companie of Spire, reported that a young man at shrift madd lamentable moane unto him for the like losse. But his gravitie suffered him not to beleeve lightlie any such reports, and therefore made the young man untrusse his codpeece pointe, and sawe the complaint to be true and just. Whereupon he advised, or rather injoined the youth to go to the witch whome he suspected, and with flattering words to intreat hir to be so good unto him as to restore him his instrument. Which by that meanes he obtained, and soon after returned to shew himselfe thankfull, and told the holie father of his good successe in that behalfe. But he so beleeved him as he would needs be *oculatus testis,* and made him pull downe his breeches, and so was satisfied of the troth and certaintie thereof.

Another yoong man being in that verie taking, went to a witch for the restitution thereof, who brought him to a tree, where she shewed him a nest and bad him clime up and take it. And being in the top of the tree, he tooke out a mightie great one and shewed the same to hir, asking hir if he might not have the same. Naie (quoth she) that is our parish preests toole, but take anie other which thou wilt. And it is there affirmed that some have found 20, and some 30 of them in one nest, being there preserved with provender as it were, or the racke and manger, with this note, wherein there is no contradiction (for all must be true that is written against witches) that if a witch deprive one of his privities, it is done onlie by prestigious meanes, so as the senses are but illuded. Marie by the divell it is reallie taken away, and in like manner restored. These are no jests, for they be written by them that were and are judges upon the lives and deaths of those persons.

—*Discoverie of Witchcraft,* IV. iv

36. Cures for Bewitchment of the Private Parts

For direct cure to such as are bewitched in their privie members, the first and speciall is confession. Then follow in a row holie water and those ceremoniall trumperies, *Ave Maries,* and all manner of crossings, which are all said to be wholesome, except the witchcraft be perpetuall, and in that case the wife maie have a divorce of course.

Item, the eating of a haggister or pie helpeth one bewitched in that member.

Item, the smoke of the tooth of a dead man.

Item, to annoint a man's bodie over with the gall of a crow.

Item, to fill a quill with quicke silver and laie the same under the cushine, where such a one sitteth, or else to put it under the threshold of the doore of the house or chamber where he dwelleth.

Item, to spet into your owne bosome if you are so bewitched is verie good.

Item, to pisse through a wedding ring. If you would know who is hurt in his privities by witchcraft, and who otherwise is therein diseased, Hostiensis answereth. But so as I am ashamed to english it, and therefore have here set down his experiment in Latin. *Quando nullatenus movetur, & nunquam potuit cognoscere; hoc est signum frigiditatis sed quando movetur & erigitur, perficere autem non potest, est signum maleficii.*

But Sir Th. Moore hath such a cure in this matter as I am

ashamed to write either in Latine or English. For in filthie bawderie it passeth all the tales that ever I heard. But that is rather a medicine to procure generation than the cure of witchcraft, though it serve both turnes.
—*Discoverie of Witchcraft*, IV. viii

37. A Charm for the Toothache

A charme for the headache: Tie a halter about your head wherewith one hath beene hanged.
—*Discoverie of Witchcraft*, XII, xiv

* * *

The interrogation and trial of Joan of Arc make fascinating reading, but I dare not go into the subject here because first, to do it justice I should have to give it far more space than any anthology could reasonably be expected to spare, and second, because it would open so many questions that the commentary on them would seem (for our present purposes) interminable. But one small excerpt I must include, first because it justifies mentioning the African Joan who follows, but more important, because I dare not really omit something about the so-called "fairy folk," the goblins that are so firmly rooted in European tradition.

For they existed; there seems little question about it. They were the medieval (and later) equivalents of our gypsies, bands of dark, small men and women who lived in mound dwellings on the fringes of rural communities. They stole from farmers. Sometimes they traded food for small tools and implements. Sometimes they kidnapped children, and to claim a "fairy" for mother was by no means uncommon. Richard Coeur de Lion had a "demon mother." But most important of all, they seem to have retained an Iron Age memory of the efficacy of certain herbs, of certain forms of pre-Christian magic of which their more settled contemporaries were much in awe. It has struck me that the magical white powder given away in No. 40 may very well have been penicillin.

38. From the Trial of Joan of Arc

Not far from Domremy there stands a tree that is called *Arbor Dominarum,* or Tree of Women. Some call it the Fairies' Tree. Nearby there is a spring. It is an enormous tree, a beech from which mayleaves grow, and it belongs to the Seigneur de Bourlemont. Old folk, not of Joan's family, said that fairy people used to walk there. Indeed, she had heard her godmother Jeanne, the Mayor's wife, tell how she had met fairy people there, though she (Joan) had never seen any.

She had used to make posies there with other girls for the Blessed Mary of Domremy. Now and then she had joined other girls in hanging garlands on the tree. Sometimes they left them there, and sometimes not. As a child she had danced there with others, but not since she had reached womanhood. She had sung songs there more often than she had danced. She had heard it said that she became conscious of her mission at the fairy tree. The saints came and spoke to her at the spring nearby, but when she was asked if they came to the tree itself she would not reply.

She denied having a mandrake, but knew there was one near the tree.

My godmother (she said), who saw fairies was an honest woman, not a clairvoyant or a witch.

She did not hang wreaths on the tree in honour of Saints Katherine and Margaret.

She had never had intercourse with or known anything about those who flew through the air with fairies. She had heard they came on Thursdays, but thought it was probably witchcraft.

—JULES ETIENNE JOSEPH QUICHERAT,
Procès de condemnation et de rehabilitation de Jeanne d'Arc,
Paris, 1841

39. A Barotse Joan of Arc

The young [Barotse] girl is not the *vivandière* of the army. She is its prophetess. She has been chosen by the clairvoyant's *astragali* to interpret for the gods, and nothing is done unless she has ordered it. She gives the signal to march; she signals when to halt. In her horn she carries the medicines they will need—and the charms. She moves always in the van, and even when the soldiers are resting no one may walk in front of her. If she is tired or ill, young soldiers must carry her. When they meet the enemy she fires the first shot, and no matter how long the action goes on she may neither eat nor sleep nor drink nor even sit down. . . . And in return, when the army finally comes home, she will be made a *maori*, one of the king's wives.

—*Missions evangéliques*, lxiii

40. A White Witch in Yorkshire

There was (he saith) as I have heard the story credibly reported in this Country (Yorkshire), a Man apprehended for suspicion of Witchcraft. He was of that sort we call white Witches, which are such as do cures beyond the ordinary reasons and deductions of our usual practitioners, and are supposed (and most part of them truly) to do the same by ministration of spirits (from whence . . . most Sciences at first grow) and therefore are by good reason provided against by our Civil Laws, as being ways full of danger and deceit, and scarce ever otherwise obtained than by a devillish compact of the exchange of ones Soul to that assistant spirit for the honour of Mountebankery.

What this man did was with a white powder which, he said, he received from the Fairies, and that going to a Hill he knocked three times, and the Hill opened, and he had access to and conversed with a visible people, and offered that if any Gentleman present would either go himself in person, or send his servant, he would conduct them thither, or show them the place and persons from whom he had his skill.

To this I shall only add thus much, that the man was accused for invoking and calling upon evil spirits, and was a very simple and illiterate person to any mans judgement, and had been formerly very poor, but had gotten some pretty little means to maintain himself, his Wife and diverse small children by his cures done with this white powder, of which there were sufficient proofs, and the Judge asking him how he came by the powder, he told a story to this effect.

That one night before day was gone, as he was going home from his labour, being very sad and full of heavy thoughts, not knowing how to get meat and drink for his Wife and Children, he met a fair Woman in fine cloaths who asked him why he was so sad, and he told her it was by reason of his poverty. To which she said that if he would follow her counsel she would help him to that which would serve to get him a good living.

To which he said he would consent with all his heart, so it were not by unlawful ways. She told him it should not be by any such ways, but by doing of good and curing of sick people. And so warning him strictly to meet her there the next night at the same time, she departed from him and he went home.

And the next night at the time appointed he duly waited, and she (according to promise) came and told him it was well he came so duly, otherwise he had missed of that benefit that she intended to do unto him, and so bade him follow her and not be afraid.

Thereupon she led him to a little Hill, and she knocked three times and the Hill opened. And they went in and came to a fair hall, wherein was a Queen sitting in great state, and many people about her. And the Gentlewoman that brought him presented him to the Queen. And she said he was welcome, and bid the Gentlewoman give him some of the white powder and teach him how to use it, which she did, and gave him a little wood box full of the white powder, and bad him give 2 or 3 grain of it to any that were sick, and it would heal them. And so she brought him forth of the Hill, and so they parted.

And being asked by the Judge whether the place within the Hill, which he called a Hall, were light or dark, he said indifferent, as it is with us in the twilight. And being asked how he got more powder, he said when he wanted he went to that Hill and knocked three times, and said every time, "I am coming, I am coming." Whereupon it opened, and he going in was conducted by the aforesaid Woman to the Queen, and

so had more powder given him. This was the plain and simple story (however it may be judged of) that he told before the Judge and the whole Court and the Jury. And there being no proof but what cures he had done to very many, the Jury did acquit him.
—JOHN WEBSTER, *Displaying of Supposed Witchcraft,*
London, 1677

41. Aboriginal Medicine with Quartz Crystals

During the first years of European colonization in the Brisbane district . . . nearly all aches, pains and diseases were ascribed to the quartz crystal in the possession of some medicine man (*turrwan*). This crystal gave its owner supernatural powers. The spirit of the *turrwan* used to put the crystal into the victim, who could only be cured by getting a medicine man to suck it out again; thus a medicine man could make an individual sick even when he was miles away, and 'doom' him, so to speak.
—DR. W. E. ROTH, *North Queensland Ethnology,* 1907

* * *

Witches were never "possessed." But innocent victims were, and in the seventeenth century, nuns of several orders as well as many children in orphanages are said to have been possessed by the devil at the instigation of witches and wizards. The hysterical children of Salem, Massachusetts, in 1692 were "possessed," and caused the deaths of many quite harmless men and women, and I shall have more to say about all this in a moment. But first I want to set down several cases of possession in more primitive peoples, for hysteria, and indeed contagious hysteria, are by no means confined to those who have been isolated from the general community or to individuals under some form of psychic stress. The "demon" who possesses is older than written history. He is to be found in all cultures, and indeed in all religions.

42. An Elephant Possessed of the Devil

During a hunting expedition, a somewhat influential chief named Nkoba was overtaken by a wounded female elephant who, lifting him from the ground with her trunk . . . impaled him on one of her tusks. . . . Terrible was the wailing of his adherents. . . . The whole district was assembled before the *nganga nkissi*, who was to pronounce whether the elephant was possessed of the devil or had been bewitched by some enemy of the dead chief or whether it was a case of *diambudi nzambi*, the will of the Great Spirit.
—H. WARD, *Five Years with the Congo Cannibals*, 1890

43. Congolese Evil Spirits

Perhaps when the sun is overhead to-day, you may be drinking palm wine with a man, unconscious that he is possessed of an evil spirit, in the evening you hear the cry of "Nkole! Nkole!" (crocodile) and you know that one of these monsters, lurking in the muddy waters near the river bank, has grabbed a poor victim who had come to fill a water jar. At night you are awakened from your sleep by the alarmed cackling in your hen-house, and you will find that your stock of poultry has been decreased by a visit from a *muntula* (bush cat). Now . . . the man with whom you drank palm wine, the crocodile who snatched an unwary villager from the river bank, and the stealthy little robber of your hens are one and the same individual, possessed of an evil spirit.
—E. J. GLAVE, *Six Years of Adventure in Congo Land*, 1893

44. The Abyssinian Boudah

It often happens in Abyssinia that people seem possessed by an evil spirit. The Abyssinians call it *boudah*. I witnessed these wonderful and dark occurrences many times, but will relate one only—and even in this case I must not describe the most horrible and disgusting details.

One evening when I was in my house at Gaffat, a woman began to cry out fearfully and run up and down the road on her hands and feet like a wild beast, quite unconscious of what she was doing. The people said to me, "This is the *boudah,* and if it is not driven out of her she will die." A large number of people gathered round her, and many means were tried, but all in vain. She was always howling and roaring in an unnatural and most powerful voice. At length a man was called, a blacksmith by profession, of whom it was said that he was in secret connection with the evil spirit. He called the woman, who obeyed him at once. He took her hand in his and dropped the juice of the white onion or garlic into her nose, and said to her—or rather to the evil spirit who possessed her, "Why didst thou possess this poor woman?" "Because I was allowed to do so."

"What is thy name?"

"My name is Gebroo."

"Where is thy country?"

"My country is Godjam."

"How many people didst thou take possession of?"

"I took possession of forty people, men and women."

"Now I command thee to leave this woman."

"I will leave her on one condition."

"What is that condition?"

"I want to eat the flesh of a donkey."

"Very well," said the man. "Thou mayest have that."

So a donkey was brought which had a wounded back from carrying heavy loads, and its back was quite sore and full of matter. The woman then ran upon the donkey and bit the flesh out of the poor creature's back. But though the donkey kicked and ran off, she did not fall down, but clung to it just as if she were nailed on the animal's back.

The man called the woman back to him, and said to the evil spirit, "Now art thou satisfied?"

"Not yet," was the reply, and a disgusting mixture was asked for, which was prepared for the woman and put down in a secret place which she could not see. But when the man said, "Go and look for your drink," she ran up on all fours like an animal and drank the whole potful to the very last drop.

Then she came back to the man, who said again, "Now take up this stone." It was a very large stone which she would not have been able to move in her natural condition, but she took it up with ease upon her head, and turned round like a wheel until the stone flew off on one side and she was on the other on the ground.

The man then said, "Take her now away to bed, for the *boudah* has left her." The poor woman slept for about ten hours, and then awoke and went to her work, and did not know anything of that which had passed over her, nor what she did and said.

—THEOPHILUS WALDMEIER, *Autobiography*, London, 1886

* * *

The devils of Loudun are famous. Those of Louviers and Sainte-Baume are less familiar to us, chiefly because they have not yet been turned into popular entertainment. But the possession of Madeleine de la Palud (Michaëlis calls her Magdalene Demandouls) is one of the most vivid and best documented in the whole of the seventeenth century. And yet Michaëlis' book, his Admirable Historie, *has not been reprinted since 1613, and as far as I know there are only five copies of it in all England.*

The story can be told very briefly. The Provençal priest, Louis Gauffridi, was a traveler, a mystic, a mountaineer, a most agreeable preacher, and seems in addition to have had considerable power over women. In about 1605 a slender, fair-haired girl of twelve, daughter of a well-to-do family and named Madeleine de la Palud was put in his care. Madeleine was vain, precocious, impressionable, highly emotional, and possessed of an intense sexuality. Gauffridi seduced her. He seems to have told her that since he could not marry her in the sight of God he would do so in the sight of the devil. He gave her a silver ring engraved with cabalistic signs, and it is likely that he took her to a Sabbat and there celebrated a mass on her naked body. Then, either to ensure her silence, or else to make access easy, he had her entered as a novice in the Ursuline convent near Sainte-Baume. But there Madeleine began to be subject to terrible fits of depression. Whether Gauffridi was caught with her flagrante delicto, or whether the love-sick girl simply boasted that she was Beelzebub's mistress we do not know. But in very short order the convent was seized with what has aptly been called sheer, midsummer madness. A nun called Louise Capeau caught the infection and had to have three devils exorcised out of her. A Flemish exorcist was brought in, a certain Dr. Dompt; the renowned inquisitor, Sebastian Michaëlis, came down to investigate the phenomena. Madeleine and Louise were taken into custody and surrounded by large numbers of guards and ecclesiastics who preached at, confessed, and exorcised them by the hour. It would have been enough to drive a sane woman mad. We ourselves find it difficult to imagine the inner constraint, the huge, rending sense of guilt with which they must have been oppressed. Devils lurked in the very walls and listened to the hour-long sermons. Beelzebub mocked. He spoke in his own voice out of Madeleine's mouth, and said awful, shocking words she could not wittingly have said. Her body shook until it had to be held down. She no longer knew who she was, the devil or Gauffridi, the wizard, a nun, an innocent girl or a naked mistress taking an outrageous pleasure in being debauched. They stretched her on a pallet and examined her breasts, her private parts and her feet (she was proud of her feet) for the devil's marks. As chief inquisitor, Michaëlis himself probed her vagina in the interests of ecclesiastical truth, and discovered perhaps to his relief and satisfaction that she was not a virgin.

They anathematized her, cleric after learned cleric, and for hours on end, as "miserable, accursed, damned," they quoted scriptural authority for every one of their maledictions and pleas for her reconversion, and during a period of five months, during a long, cold winter while the inquisition continued in those gloomy rooms, she tossed from pillar to post, defied and pleaded with them in turn, swung from God to the devil. She danced lewd dances, shouted, and tried to escape, starved herself, was put on exhibition, exposed her body, fainted until they thought she had died, expressed with almost every word her almost overwhelming sexual desire and sense of guilt.

Seen in the light of modern psychiatric knowledge, her ordeal looks to have been all but intolerable. Yet Michaëlis gives frequent signs that he finds her attractive. He confronts her with Gauffridi to see how she will react. Then Gauffridi is taken into an adjoining room, stripped for examination (they are looking for the devil's marks), and the examiners turn their heads away in embarrassment. He has an erection. Madeleine is immured in a charnel house to find out if this will bring her to her senses. But I must let the interrogation speak for itself. Out of many hundred pages I have taken a few. On the 30th of April, 1611, Gauffridi was burned at the stake. Madeleine was nineteen years old.

45. The Possession of Madeleine de la Palud

19 Jan. 1611. Madeleine deposes: They provide a banquet, setting three tables according to the three diversities of the people above named (hags and witches, sorcerers and sorceresses, magicians). They do have the charge of bread, doe bring in bread made of corne which invisibly they pilfer and steale from divers places. The drink which they have is Malmesy to provoke and prepare the flesh to luxurious wantonness: and this liquor is brought by certain deputed for that purpose from sellers whence they steale the same. The meate they ordinarily eate is the flesh of young children, which they cooke and make ready in the Synagogue, sometimes bringing them thither alive by stealing them from those houses where they have opportunity to come. They have no use of knives at table for feare least they should bee laid a crosse, and emblematically to shew that they must not cut off the foreskin of their damnable customes and habits; and it may be also to avoide the massacring of one another in the Sabbath by reason of some enmity or hatred. They have also no salt, which figureth out wisdome and understanding;

neither know they the use of olives or oyle which represent mercy.

When this is done, the Magicians and those that can reade sing certain Psalmes . . . transferring all to the praise of Lucifer and the Divels. And the Hagges and Sorcerers doe howle and vary their hellish cries high and low, counterfeiting a kind of villanous musicke. They also daunce at the sound of Viols and other instruments, which were brought thither by those that were skild to play upon them. Finally they committed uncleannesse one with another. Upon Sundaies they pollute themselves by their filthy copulation with Divels that are Succubi and Incubi. Upon Thursdaies they contaminate themselves with Sodomy and upon Saturdaies they doe prostitute themselves to abominable bestiality: upon other daies they use the ordinary course which nature prompteth unto them.

20 Jan. It happened towards the evening at the time wherein Magdalene was accustomed to come to S. Baume to be exorcised, they found her stiffe as a statue of marble in all her limmes, and very dull and drowsie, so that they were forced to carry her between foure to the church, where shee remained a good space at the foote of the high Altar and could not be brought to her selfe till they carried her to the place of the blessed Penitence, applying and laying the holy Pix upon her face. Whereupon she came to her selfe and went forth to be exorcised.

22 Jan. After dinner Belzebub committed many outrages in her chamber, dauncing and singing, and within a while he ranne suddenly, and having opened the doore, he made Magdalene to runne very nimbly towards the great gate of S. Baume, but she was presently followed and taken.

Afterward, Belzebub being exorcised with the stole to make answer why hee had so done, at length replyed that the Magician Lewes and his lieutenant stayed for her at the fountaine to the end that they might transport her together with themselves if she would yeeld consent thereunto, pretending they would give her a charme to that purpose. And this happened three or foure several times.

25. Jan. At first Belzebub refuses to answer questions, but at length he spake in the eare of the Priest as (though) unwilling to be heard. The Synagogue adored the picture of Magdalene as of a Princesse, which was set in the same place where her self was wont to sit in the Synagogue, and al reverence was performed to her supposed presence as if she had been really present, all which was done to moove her to returne unto them, considering the honour which they did her picture . . . Being demanded whether or no they conceived it not to be a great madnesse to adore a mortall and corruptible creature carying nothing but durt and excrement within her, who must shortly also die when it pleased God, hee there-upon turned aside his face and answered nothing.

We have to understand that when the dead speaks, it is through Madelein's lips. When he turns aside his head, it is Madeleine's head that has been turned aside.

27 Jan. She was long questioned. Then towards the evening Magdalene fell a singing and dancing and playing many tricks in the chamber, so that they threatened to carry her to the holy house and Penance, which being done, Belzebub made her sleep so soundly as if she had been dead for the space of three or foure houres. At last, after many prayers, Psalmes, Litanies and Exorcisms, fetching a deepe sigh she began to awake, affirming that the Magician had againe inchanted her, and would have strangled her. And indeed she was like to die at that instant, feeling herself extremely perplexed. Yet recommending her selfe to God, the Divels power ceased, and howbeit the night before, whiles they held their assembly, the Magician had presented himselfe unto her upon his knee with an halter about his neck, praying her to returne unto him, not to discover him and the other Magicians, and in her presence had adored her statue all gilded over, drawing bloud out of the hands of the Witches with rasors and saying unto her, "Behold what honour wee would do your person, considering wee doe so much to your picture. Yet would shee by no meanes yeeld her consent, but remained victorious . . . Magdalene added that the Magician, seeing her continue in her constancy, cryed out, saying to the whole company, "Is there any heere present that would die for her?" And presently there presented himselfe a young man, declaring that himselfe was

ready for that purpose. Whom the Magician twice stabbed with a poniard. Yet would shee by meanes yeeld her consent.

30 Jan. At night at the entrance of the Exorcismes, Belzebub began to torment Magdalene in fearfull manner, causing her to tremble [in] every joint, and making her head to trumble some-while backwards and againe suddenly forward, even to her belly, beating the earth with both her hands, in so much as they were inforced to put a cushion upon the ground for her to beat upon. Notwithstanding, she still vexed herselfe, and this continued for the space of above halfe an houre.

1 March. He cryed, saying "I renounce Paradise in the behalfe of Lewes Gaufridy. I renounce the Trinity, the Father, the Sonne and the holy Ghost in the behalfe of Lewes Gaufridy. I renounce the Eucharist, all holy Inspirations, all the members of Jesus Christ," naming them all from the head to the feet, and particularly renouncing every particular member, "all the Masses and Prayers" which were said for him, and every thing that might serve as a means for his salvation. . . .

Thus (she) continued all the dayes following, during which time the Magician Lewes was brought to the Chappel, to the end he might understand the renouncements which Belzebub made in his behalfe. And as Lewes beheld Magdalene thus tormented of the Divel, Belzebub, turning himselfe towards him, said, "Come hither, my friend, and see if I doe not torment her as much as thou desirest. . . ."

At evening he was visited by the three Phisitians, Fonetine, Merindol and Crassy, and two Chirurgeons, Pontemps and Prouet, and having stripped him in the presence of Theron and Garandeau, the forenamed Commissioners, they found him in a shamefull and odious fashion, whereat they were ashamed themselves, and turned their faces aside. . .

The selfe same Saturday at the confronting of the one against the other, Magdalene said unto the Magician . . . "Thou canst but not remember how thou diddest abuse my body, and take away my virginity at my fathers house in Marseilles . . . how thou diddest lead me to the Synagogue, and with thine own hand diddest baptise me in the name of the Divell, and annoint me with their execrable

Chrisome, causing me to renounce God and my portion in Paradise, and to make all other renouncements which they use to do in Synagogue. Thou diddest also stampe the Divels markes upon me, which I still carry in my body. Thirdly, thou hast given me an Agnus Dei and a peach charmed . . . To these accusations Lewes the Magician made answere that they are all false.

10 March. The Devil made her decide to starve herself. He pulled her from the table and wracked her in a horrible manner, wresting backward her legs and armes and making her bones to crack and grate one against the other, and making her fingers crooke sundry ways, which indured sometimes for the space of halfe an houre, sometimes a quarter of an houre, and sometimes an houre. And this terrible handling continued till the end of Aprill . . . There also came much people of the best note in the citty of Aix at the time when Magdalene used to dine and sup, purposely to see this spectacle.

One day after dinner a Ladie brought her some drage (sugared?) powder and some Syrope to give her to drinke, but the Divell would never pemit her, shutting up her teeth and saying, "All these things are too, too nourishing."

17 March. In the Chapel which is called the Chapel of S. Saviour, and in the most private part of all the Church and the most closely kept, there was a Reliquary locked with a key, where there were many bones decently and reverently ranked, and no man knew what it was, but that there was a likelyhood that it might be the Relicks of Saints. The said Girandeau was of opinion to have her that was possessed to be brought thither and to exorcise her in that very place, to see the countenance and portment of the Divell.

Being come thither, they tooke two skulls, one of a lesser size and another greater, and applyed them one after the other unto her that was possessed. Whereupon she wagged her head from one side to the other, and could not stand quyet, but ever said, "Take this away."

27 March. After dinner Belzebub made Magdalene take a knife and set it against her breast, tempting her to kill her selfe with her owne hand. When the knife was taken away, he caused her to lay hold on her owne throate, and would have strangled her if they had not hindered him.

7 April. Father Romillon was of opinion that it was fit to cut close Magdalene's haire, because shee tooke such delight in the yellow and golden colour of the same. Whereat Belzebub was exceeding angry and tormented her without intermission all the time of the Exorcismes, making her to plunge with her head downe to the ground, and by a continual forced motion to bow it arch-wise, sometimes forward and sometimes backward, and constrained her to beate her face with her fist, saying, "I will teach thee to cut thy haire, for I took this hold [*i.e.*, took hold of it]. Where shall I next betake my selfe?"

The next ensuing time about midnight the Divels did forceably cause her to tumble and leape that so they might get her out of the chamber where they that watched with her did lye. But it was perceived by Father Francis Billet who caused her to return. Yet when he was departed to take his rest, the Divels would have caryed her through the chimney, and she was found with her head up against the wall of the chimney as though she had been by violence lifted up thither.

—Sebastian Michaëlis, *Admirable Historie of the Possession and Conversion of a Penitent Woman,* London, 1613

* * *

Gauffridi was brought to trial, and on the 30th of April the verdict was handed down.

The Court hath and doth declare the said Lewes Gaufridy attainted, guiltie and convicted of the cases and crimes aforesaid, wherewith-all he hath been burthened: and to make some amends and reparation for the same, the said Court hath and doth condemne him to be delivered up into the hands of the Executioner for matters capitall, and to bee lead thorow all the usuall streetes and quarters of the citie of Aix, and before the great gate of the Metropolitan·Church of S. Saviour to performe this penance, that is, to goe thither bare-headed and bare-footed with a linke burning in his hand and a rope about his necke, and upon his knees to aske forgiveness of God, the King and Justice.

Which being performed, he is to be brought to the place of

Preaching in the said towne, and there to be burnt alive in a pile of wood (which shall be prepared for the purpose) untill his bodie and bones be consumed and burned to ashes, which are also afterward to be scattered and cast into the winde, and all his goods and everie parcell thereof to be seazed upon and confiscated to the King.

And before he be executed, hee shall be tortured and put upon the racke both after the ordinarie and extraordinarie manner, to force from his mouth the true detection of his complices.

> *In the ultimate torture, the* question extraordinaire, *the prisoner has his arms tied behind his back at the wrists. Then the rope securing them is drawn over a pulley secured as high above him as can practically be managed. Weights are tied to his feet and he is drawn up until he has reached the pulley. Then suddenly the rope is allowed to go slack. Down he plummets. But he is stopped with a jerk before his feet have quite reached the ground.*

46. The Tariff for Torture in Cologne

		Thaler	Albus
1.	For tearing apart and quartering by four horses,	5	5
2.	For quartering	4	0
3.	For the necessary rope for this purpose	1	0
4.	For hanging the four quarters in four corners, necessary rope, nails, chains and transport included	5	26
5.	For beheading and burning, all incl.	5	26
6.	For the necessary rope for this procedure, and for preparing and igniting stake	2	0
7.	For strangling and burning	4	0
8.	For rope and for preparing and igniting stake	2	0
9.	For burning alive	4	0
10.	For breaking alive on the wheel	4	0

		Thaler	Albus
11.	For rope and chains for this procedure	2	0
12.	For setting up body tied to wheel	2	52
13.	For beheading only	2	52
14.	For necessary cloth to cover face and for necessary rope	1	0
15.	For digging hole and burying corpse	1	26
16.	For beheading and tying body to wheel	4	0
17.	For cutting off a hand or several fingers and beheading, all together	2	26
18.	Same incl. burning with hot iron	1	26
19.	For beheading and sticking head on pole	3	26
20.	For hanging	2	52
21.	For rope, chain and nails needed for the purpose	1	26
22.	Before execution, for squeezing criminal with red hot tongs, for each application		26
23.	For cutting out tongue or part thereof, and afterward for burning mouth with red hot iron	5	0
24.	For nailing cut off tongue or hand to gallows	1	26
25.	For flogging in gaol, incl. rods	1	0
26.	For inspecting prisoner after branding	0	26
27.	For arranging and crushing thumb	0	26
28.	For second degree torture, incl. setting limbs afterward	2	26
29.	For daily food	1	26
30.	For each assistant	0	30
31.	For hiring horse, incl. stable and fodder, per day	1	26

All vouchers and accounts to be submitted to the Archbishop's Treasury.

Bonn, 15th January, 1757

—*Tariff for Torture approved for the Archbishopric of Cologne, 1757. From* RUSSELL HOPE ROBBINS, *Encyclopedia of Witchcraft and Demonology,* New York, 1959

* * *

It is time now to come to the relationship of witches with the devil himself, to the Sabbat, the feasting, the dancing, the *fornication. And depositions are there aplenty. Some were no doubt extracted under torture. But torture was illegal in England, and in fact was not often practiced. Even so, the statements are so similar—in France, in England, in Scotland—that it seems unlikely they could all have been invented. They reflect actual happenings. And indeed, they furnish such a wealth of unlikely detail that many of them bear all the marks of truth. There were Sabbats, and the devil (in many shapes) made love to the women who attended them. Even when copulation was painful (he seems sometimes to have been fitted with an artificial phallus), they went back again and again to give themselves. Even at the foot of the gallows there were those who cried out to get the hanging over quickly so they could hurry down to hell and take their pleasures over and over again.*

47. Elspeth Reoch Meets the Devil

1616. Elspeth Reoch of Orkney: she confessed that when she was a young lass of twelve years of age or thereabouts, and had wandered out of Caithness where she was born to Lochaber she came to Allan McKeldowie's wife who was her aunt. One day, being away from the loch in the country, she had returned and was waiting at the loch side for the boat to come and fetch her, when two men approached her, one clad in black, and the other with a green tartan plaid about him. And that the man with the plaid said to her she was a pretty one, and he would teach her to know and see whatever she should desire. And thereafter, within two years she bore her first child, and when she had been delivered in her sister's house, the black man came to her that had first come to her at Lochaber. And he called himself a fairy man. On Yule day she confessed that the devil, whom she calls a fairy man, lay with her.

—*Maitland Club Miscellany,* II

48. Copulation with the Devil

It is well known that every witch who copulates with the devil (and they all do this when they accept him as their Master) agrees that if his organ ejaculates semen it is so cold that it makes them shiver when it enters their bodies. *Boguet reports the confession of Jacquema Paget that* she had often taken the devil's penis in her hand when he lay with her. It was as cold as ice, a good finger long, but not as thick as a man's. *De Lancre records the confession of Jeannette d'Abadie, aged sixteen, that* she always dreaded the devil's approach *(he had first lain with her when she was a virgin)*, because his member was scaly and caused her considerable pain, besides which his semen was cold, unlike that of other men at the Sabbat, which was naturally pleasant. "He requires us to kiss his face," she said, "then his navel, this his penis, then his arse."

In North Berwick, "Efter that the Devell had endit his admonitions, he cam down out of the pulpit and caused all the company to com and kiss his ers, quilk they said was cauld lyk yce." *Isobel Gowdie confessed that* he is abler for us that way than any man can be, only he was heavie lyk a malt sack, a hudg nature, verie cold, as yce. *Janet Breadheid called him* a meikle, blak, roch man, werie cold; and I found his nature als cold within me as spring well-water. *Nicholas Remy states that* all witches affirm that the devil's virile member is so large and so terribly stiff that they cannot take it into them without great pain. Alexée Dragaea said in Lorraine in 1598 that the devil's penis was as mighty at rest as when it was standing; it was as long as the handle of an oven fork, but she had not noticed any scrotum or testicles. Claude Fellet reported on the 2nd of November, 1584, that it had looked to her like a spindle hugely enlarged, so that even the widest woman could not take it in without pain. Nicolle Morèle (19th January, 1587) testified that after such fornication she always had to take to her bed. One Didatia, who came from Miremont, confessed on the 31st of July, 1588, that she had known many men, but that whenever she took in the devil's enormous phallus the sheets were soaked in blood. *Sylvine de* la Plaine *reported in 1616, according to De Lancre, that* the devil's member was like that of a horse and went in, cold as ice. The jet of its semen was very cold too, and when he withdrew it scratched and burned like fire.

But Madame Bourignon (she kept an orphanage) reported that her girls copulated daily with the devil, went to the Sabbat, ate, drank, danced and ended the night with all sorts of whorishness. *Nor did they want to stop. One girl of twenty-two said to her* I would not change for anything. I am too happy. I am perpetually being caressed. *A twelve-year-old said that* her devil was a boy hardly older than she. He was her lover and lay with her every night. *As for Rebecca West, the devil came to her house just as she was going to bed. He* told her he would marry her, and that shee could not deny him. Shee said he kissed her, but was as cold as clay, and married her that night in this manner. He tooke her by the hand and lead her about the chamber, and promised to be her loving husband till death and to avenge her of her enemies. And that then she promised him to be his obedient wife till death, and to deny God and Christ Jesus. *But of little Jonet Howat, who first went to the Sabbat when she was seven, the devil said* "What shall I do with such a little bairn as she?"

—A Miscellany *from the* Demonolatry and other sources

49. The Devil and Pacts with Children

The devils never make pacts of any kind with children or allow them to take their vows until they have reached the age of puberty . . . Magdalene de la Croix, Abbess of Moniale in Cordova confessed that Satan never copulates with, or has carnal knowledge of those who have not reached the age of twelve years.

—Jean Bodin, *De la Demonomanie des Sorciers,* Rouen, 1604

50. Reginald Scot on the Sabbat

Danaeus saith the divell oftentimes in the likenes of a sumner meeteth them at markets and faires and warneth them to appeere in their assemblies at a certeine houre in the night, that he may understand whom they have slaine and how they have profited.

If they be lame, he saith the divell delivereth them a staffe to convey them thither invisiblie through the aire; and that then they fall a dansing and singing of bawdie songs, wherein he leadeth the danse himselfe. Which danse, and other conferences being ended, he supplieth their wants of powders and roots to intoxicate withall, and giveth to everie novice a marke, either with his teeth or with his clawes. And so they kisse the divels bare buttocks and depart, not forgetting every daie afterwards to offer to him dogs, cats, hens or bloud of their owne.

And all this doth Danaeus report as a troth, and as it were, upon his owne knowledge. And yet else-where he saith: In these matters they doo but dreame, and doo not those things indeed which they confesse through their distemperature, (the) growing of their melancholie humor. And therefore (saith he) these things which they report of themselves are but meere illusions.

Psellus addeth hereunto that certeine magical hereticks, to wit, the *Eutychians*, assemblie themselves everie good fridaie at night, and putting out the candles, doo commit incestuous adulterie, the father with the daughter, the sister with the brother and the sonne with the mother. And the ninth month they returne and are delivered, and cutting their children in peeces, fill their pots with their bloud. Then burne they the carcasses and mingle the ashes therewith, and so preserve the same for magicall purposes.

Cordanus writeth (though in mine opinion not verie probablie) that these excourses, dansings, &c. had their beginning from certain heretikes called *Dulcini*, who devised these feasts of Bacchus which are named *Orgia*, whereunto these kind of people openlie assembled, and beginning with

riot, ended with this follie. Which feasts being prohibited, they nevertheles hanted them secretlie. And when they could not doo so, then did they in cogitation onelie. And even to this daie (saith he) there remaineth a certeine image or resemblance thereof among our melancolike women.
—*Discoverie of Witchcraft*, III. iii

* * *

Perhaps to give more credit to Scot's mockery of such ceremonies (for he thought them nothing but wishful thinking), I should here include an extract from the work of a traveler in eastern Russia. According to him, the wish was there the father to fulfillment.

51. Love Magic in Kamtchatcha

If a man wishes for a girl's love, all he need do is tell her that he dreamed she was in love with him. It becomes in her mind a mortal sin to refuse herself, for if she did, she might die. If someone needs a *kuklanda* or a *barka*, or anything else which he cannot afford, he need only say, "Last night I dreamed that I was sleeping in your *kuklanda*," and at once the other replies, "Take it. It is no longer mine." For he is perfectly certain that if he does not give the object away he will lose his life.

—G. H STELLER, *Beschreibung von dem Lande Kamtschalka*, 1704

52. The Deposition of Silvain Neuillon

The Arrest and the Charges brought by the prosecutor of Orleans against Silvain Neuillon, Gentian le Clerc, called

"Nivelle," and Mathurin Ferrand of the village of Nouen in Sologne, convicted of witchcraft on the 20th of June, 1614.

Friday, the 20th of June, 1614: the interrogation of the above Neuillon, roofer and mason, aged 77 years.

The prosecutor informed him that he intended to have the hair on his body shaved and his clothes changed so that he would be forced to tell the truth. To which the answer was, "Do you want to kill me, gentlemen? If I tell you the truth, will you not have me shaved?"

He confessed that he was present at the Sabbat near Nouan at a place called Olivet.

He stated that the Sabbat was held in a certain house, and that while it was in progress he saw in front of the hearth a black man, that is, a man in black, whose head was however not visible. He saw also two goats, male and female, with thick black coats. There were some two hundred people present, all masked except for one called Ferrand. As they went forward to the sacrifice, some gave money as in church.

Opposite the black man at the fireplace, he saw another, also very big and in black, who was looking at a book. Its pages were blue and black. The man kept mumbling words between his teeth without anyone being able to understand what he was saying. A black host was raised, then a chalice made of dirty, wretched pewter. He observed those present dancing back to back, and the two goats, male and female, were in their midst.

At dinner there was meat so insipid as to be almost inedible. He believed it was horsemeat. The black man spoke as though his words were coming out of a hollow cave. There were about twelve children present in women's arms, and the devil beat one woman with a stick because she had not brought him her child as she had promised. The man in black gave the children cakes.

He deposed that those who do not attend the Sabbat have to pay a fine of 8 sous, that processions are held where he has sometimes seen six hundred people, that the two devils at the Sabbat were called Orthon and Traisnesac, and that they bowed toward those who brought children as though to thank them, and kissed the said children's arses.

He deposed that he had seen the devil in various costumes.

Sometimes he was dressed as a goat with two faces. Sometimes he was a large sheep.

He deposed that they baptized children at the Sabbat with an ointment brought by the women. They handle the penis of some man to make him ejaculate semen, and this they collect and mix with the unguent. The resulting ointment they pour on the child's head, speaking some words in Latin as they do so.

He deposed that he had seen both witches and warlocks who brought holy wafers which they had kept back at communion. The devil had made gestures of rage over these wafers, and they were afterward shredded into crumbs. Sometimes they soaked these crumbs in urine, and indeed the devil was very pleased when wafers of this sort were brought him.

He deposed that he had heard it said to Guillaume le Clerc called Nivelle that the devil gave one 8 sous for having killed a man and 5 if one had killed a woman.

He deposed that the devil beat them at the Sabbat when they could not report having done evil, and that as they went away at the end of the service he always called out, "Revenge yourselves or you will die."

He said that one could never be bewitched on a day when he had attended the (devil's) mass, or if one carried an *agnus dei* on one's person.* That one calls the host Jean le blanc, that the women sing songs in the devil's honour, and that when either sitting down at table or rising therefrom they say to the devil, "We acknowledge you for our god."

He states that the devil preaches a sermon at the Sabbat, but that no one can understand what he says because he speaks in such a growling voice, and that he throws a powder over the congregation, as in church is done with holy water.

He saw them beat water with a small stick to show how closely it resembles a hailstorm. He deposed that he often went to the Sabbat dryshod and without annointing himself, for it was madness to annoint oneself (with flying ointment) if there was not far to go.

*Four years earlier, we remember, Gauffridi was said by Madeleine to have given her an *agnus dei* and a charmed peach. It is this sort of coincidental detail that makes the stories ring true, bizarre though they sometimes sound.

He deposed that at the Sabbat the devil shows them his huge penis—as long as a candle—and that he has seen women kiss it.

He reports that witches can do no evil on a Friday because it was on that day Christ died . . .

He deposes that there are witches who keep and feed little dolls, which are devils shaped like toads, and that their food consists of a soup made out of milk and flour. At mealtime the toad is always given the first mouthful, and witches never dare leave home without asking its permission. They have to tell it how long they will be away, perhaps for three or four days. But if the familiare complains that this is too long, the witch dare not disobey or go on her journey.

When they are about to go off, whether on business or pleasure, and wish to know whether or not they will succeed in whatever they are planning, they look to see if the familiare seems happy. If it is, they go. But if it looks morose they do not so much as stir out of the house. Very often these familiars go so far as to threaten them.

When Neuillon was asked if in his opinion a judge might have such familiars arrested, seeing that they are demons, Neuillon replied that a good judge could easily deal with them, for they are frightened of good judges. But a judge who did not know his job would achieve nothing. A witch can always injure an unworthy judge, for God has abandoned him.

He deposed that he had seen incense and holy wafers taken to the Sabbat, but they did not smell wholesome as they did in a church. The devil supplied them at his services. While Tramesabot was saying mass or before he actually started, he sprinkled holy water made of urine. He always shrugged his shoulders and said, "Devil's asparagus."

Neuillon was convicted by the court of having poisoned or otherwise caused the deaths of various people and animals, and of having carried out other wicked deeds.

Gentil le Clerc deposed that his mother had first carried him to a Sabbat at the age of three, and had presented him there to a goat called Aspic. The devil had baptized him along with fourteen or fifteen others, and Jean Geraut had provided a yellow oil in a pot for a chrism. The above named

Neuillon, as well as another man called Semelle, had ejaculated semen into it, mixed it with a wooden spoon and rubbed it on their heads. He saw several people given the devil's mark—mainly women—between their breasts.

When the black man has sprinkled his holy water, each of those present throws himself to the ground as they do in church on the tombs of the dead . . . After the mass they dance. Then they copulate together, men with men and also with women. Then they sit down to table where the witness states that he has never seen salt and where there is no meat except frogs and eels. They drink no wine, only water.

Gentil le Clerc was convicted, partially hanged, then burned.*

* * *

Pierre de Lancre (1553–1631) was, with Bodin, Boguet and Nicolas Remy, one of the great French demonologists. Born in Bordeaux, the son of a vintner, he studied law both in Italy and in Bohemia, married the grandniece of Montaigne, and spent a long life investigating and prosecuting people suspected of witchcraft and demonolatry. In 1608 Henry IV sent him to investigate the witches of the Pays de Labourd. The entire population of 30,000, he discovered, priests and all, was infected. He had six hundred burned. Much of what he wrote was of course a pure feat of the imagination, either his own or that of his victims, though he would have been the first to defend his discoveries as both real and abominable. Much of what he was told had of course been extracted under torture. But again, so much is remarkably similar to the content of confessions in England, Scotland, and Germany that a large proportion of it must be—if not simple—at least adulterated truth. Unlike Bodin,

---

*I found the preceding extract printed in old French in Margaret Murray's *The Witch-Cult in Western Europe*, Oxford, 1921. But Professor Murray gave there no indication of her source for the material, and I have not been able to find any. So with this cautionary note I here offer my translation (in which I have had the assistance of Mrs. Kathleen Morris) in the hope that someone will be able to tell me where the original document is to be found.

he did not have children tortured or victims cauterized so that the flesh would putrefy before they died, or like Boguet, insist that prepubescent boys and girls be burned at the stake. But he was nevertheless one of the great bigots of his time, and like many another bigot since, died old, rich, and laden with honors.

53. The Induction of Children into the Sabbat

Witches go down on their knees and offer him small children, saying humbly, "Great Master whom I adore, I bring you this new servant who desires only to be your slave forever." And the devil replies, "You may approach."

They obey, and go forward on their knees to present the child to him. He, taking it in his arms, thanks the witch, and then giving it back, tells her to look after it well, saying that if she does so, it will add to the number of his followers.

When they are nine years old, without any fear on their part and without any violence being offered them, those terribly unfortunate children prostrate themselves in front of Satan. "What is your wish?" he asks them, looking down at them. "Do you desire to be mine?"

They reply that they do, and then he asks, "Do you come of your own free will?"

To this they agree. "In that case," he tells them, "you must do as I wish and as I do." And the great mistress or queen of the Sabbat (who is their teacher) instructs the novice who has presented himself to repeat in a loud voice, "I renounce, first God, then his Son, Jesus Christ, the Holy Ghost, the saints, the Holy Cross, the Holy Oil, my baptism, the faith I learned from my godparents, and in every respect I place myself in your power and in your hands. I do not recognize any other god, for you are my god, and I your servant."

—PIERRE DE LANCRE, *Tableau de l'inconstance des mauvais anges.* Paris, 1613

54. Young Witches Love the Devil

One witch reports that she had always thought witchcraft to be the best religion. *Jean Dibasson, aged 29, says that* the Sabbat was true paradise. One felt there a pleasure so intense it could not be expressed. Those who attend find the time too short, such pleasure and joy do they derive from it. They cannot return home again without regret, and time passes slowly indeed until the day arrives when they can go again. *Marie de la Ralde, aged 28, and according to De Lancre, an unusually beautiful woman, reports that* she felt an unusual pleasure on her way to the Sabbat, so much so that to those who happened to see her it looked as if she were on the way to her wedding. And this, not so much for the sense of freedom she felt there, or the licence (which, being modest, she claims she has neither seen nor indulged in), but because the devil so had hold of their hearts and desires that there was simply no room for any other feeling. . . . Nor did she think she was doing wrong in attending Sabbats. It simply gave her more pleasure and ease than going to mass. For the devil had made them realize that he was the true god, that the happiness they felt with him was only the foretaste of a much greater glory.

In a word, they admitted openly that they attended and witnessed all those execrable acts with a strange delight, with a mad desire to be there as often as they could. That they found the days between too long until the night they so eagerly awaited. That the waiting was too awful and the night (when it came) too short for the delight which they there experienced. When they were arrested they shed not so much as a tear, and their so-valled martyrdom, whether it is torture or the gallows, seems so delightful to them that many actually long for death. They suffer their trials with joy because they so much long to be with the devil again. Nothing makes them so impatient as the fact that they cannot demonstrate to him how eagerly they are suffering and how much they long to suffer in his name.

—*Tableau de l'inconstance*

* * *

Henri Boguet (1550–1619) was of course another of the great quadrumvirate. He was the only one who insisted on burning children because, he said, in practical terms, they were never really reformed. And he was one of the judges who insisted that his victims not be strangled before they were burned. His Discours des Sorciers, Lyons, 1608, *was twelve times reprinted in a generation. It is full of human stories, a careful, studious account of some of the many cases upon which he had passed judgment.*

55. Witches and Dancing

The witches dance in a ring back to back. The halt and the lame leap about more lightly than the others. They even encourage their companions. Now and then—but rarely—they dance by twos, sometimes side by side, but always in great confusion.

—*Discourse des Sorciers*

They dance always with their backs to the centre of the group. The girls generally dance with their hands behind them so that their bodies bend backward and their bellies protrude. Very seldom indeed do they dance one by one, that is to say, a man with one woman or girl.

—*Tableau de l'inconstance*

* * *

George Sinclair (c. 1618–1696) wrote a collection of fantastic stories about witchcraft, for he maintained that if people stopped believing in witches, then "farewell all religion, all faith, all hope of a life to come." He was among other things, a mining engineer, co-inventor of the diving bell, supervisor of the laying of Edinburgh's water pipes and professor of both philosophy and mathematics at the University of Glasgow.

56. Willaim Barton's Succubus and Death

I have reprinted my excerpts from the slightly amended edition of 1871.

About thirty years ago, more or less, there was one William Barton apprehended for Witch-Craft. His confession was first, that if he had twenty Sons he would advise them to shun the lust of uncleanness. For, said he, I never saw a beautiful Woman, Maid or Wife but I did covet them, which was the only cause that brought me to be the Devil's Vassal.

One day, says he, going from my own house in Kirkliston to the Queen's Ferry, I overtook in Dolmeny Muire a young Gentlewoman, as to appearance beautiful and comely. I drew near to her, but she shunned my company, and when I insisted, she became angry and very nyce. Said I, we are both going one way. Be pleased to accept of a convoy. At last, after much entreaty, she grew better natured, and at length came to that Familiarity that she suffered me to embrace her, and to do that which Christian ears ought not to hear of. At this time I parted from her very joyful.

The next night she appeared to him in that same very place, and after that which should not be Named, he became sensible that it was the Devil. Here he renounced his Baptism, and gave up himself to her service, and she called him her beloved and gave him this new name of John Baptist and received the Mark. She likewise bestowed fifteen pounds Scots upon him in the name of Tocher-good, and so (they) parted.

After he had gone a little way off she calls him back, and gave him a Mark-piece* in good and sufficient money which she had him spend at the Ferry, and desired him to keep entire and whole the fifteen pound, which he declared was real and true money. He confest that they never met together but they plaid their Pranks. After this confession he begged Liberty to sleep a little, which the Judges granted to him. After he had sleept a short time, he awakened with

---

*The Mark in Scotland or England was worth two-thirds of a pound.

great Laughter. The Judges inquired the reason. He replyed, being seriously urged, that the Devil had come to him and rebuked him with anger, and threatened him most furiously, that he had confessed, and bad him deny all, for he should be his warrant.

After this he turned obdured, and would never to his dying hour acknowledge any thing, for the Devil had perswaded him, even from his first ingaging that no man should take his life. Which promise he firmly believed to the very last. When they told him in the prison-house that the Fire was built and the Stake set up and the Executioner coming to bring him forth, he answered he cared not for all that. For, said he, I shall not die this day.

But the Executioner got presently orders to lead him forth, and he stepping in at the prison door in an instant shot to dead, as they say, and never stirred again. In this strait they appointed the Executioner's wife to strangle him, which she did willingly, a reward being promised to her.

When the Warlock heard this, that a woman was to put him to death, O, cryes he, how hath the Devil deceived me? Let none ever trust to his promises.

All this was done at Kirkliston before famous witnesses. The Executioner's name was Andrew Martain, and his wifes name Margaret Hamilton, who when her husband died, clapt her hands and cryed often,

Dool for this parting,
My dear Andrew Martin.

This Barton's wife had been likewise taken with him, who Declared that shew never knew him to have been a Warlock before. And she likewise declared that he never knew her to have been a Witch before. She confest that malice against one of her Neighbours moved her to ingage in the Devil's service. She renounced her Baptism and did prostrat her Body to the Foul-Spirit and received his Mark and got a new name from him, and was called Margaratus.

She was asked if she ever had any pleasure in his company. Never much, says she. But one night, going to a Dancing upon Portland-hills, he went before us in the likeness of a rough tanny-Dog, playing on a pair of Pipes. The Spring he played (says she) was *The silly bit chiken, gar cart it and pickle it and it will grow meickle.* And coming down the hill when we had done, which was the best sport, he carried the candle in his bottom under his tail, which played ey wig wag, wig wag. She was burnt with her husband.

—GEORGE SINCLAIR, *Satan's Invisible World Discovered,* Edinburgh, 1685

* * *

This seems not the sort of touch likely to have been invented. A slightly similar scene appears in the next excerpt which, for the sake of it, has been inserted slightly out of its appropriate order. Sir James Melville (1535–1617), author of the first part of it, had been page to Mary, Queen of Scots, and was entrusted with various diplomatic missions all through the minority of James VI. His often charming and voluminous memoirs were not discovered until some sixty years after his death. Robert Pitcairn, the original editor of the second section, was an early nineteenth-century antiquary. His account of Scottish criminal trials occupies six huge quarto volumes, from which certain extracts have a bearing on our subject. They appear below.

57. Witches in North Berwick

At their meeting (it was in 1590) by night in the kirk of North Berwick, the devil, clad in a black gown with a black hat upon his head, preached unto a great number of them out of the pulpit with candles lighted round about him.

—SIR JAMES MELVILLE, *Memoirs,* ed. G. Scott, 1683.

John Fian blew open the kirk doors and blew in the lights, which were like mickle black candles holden in an old man's hand round about the pulpit.

In 1594 at midnight on St. John's Eve, there appeared in a field a great Black Goat with a Candle between his Horns.

—ROBERT PITCAIRN, *Criminal Trials,* Edinburgh, 1833.

58. Feasting with the Devil

We would go to several houses in the night time. We were at Candlemas last in Granehill where we got meat and drink enough. The devil sat at the head of the table, and all the Coven about. That night he desired Alexander Elder . . . to say the grace before meat, which he did, and is this. "We eat this meat in the devil's name, etc." And then we begin to eat. And when we had ended eating we looked steadfastly to the Devil, and bowing ouselves to him, we said to him, "We thank thee, our Lord, for this.

We killed an ox in Burgie about the dawning of the day, and we brought the ox home with us to Aulderne, and did eat all amongst us in an house in Aulderne, and feasted on it.
—*Criminal Trials*

59. A Great Meeting in Loudian

In 1678 the devill had a great meeting of witches in Loudian, where among others was a warlock who had formerly been admitted to the ministrie in the presbyterian tymes, and when the bishops came in, conformed with them. But being flagitious and wicked, was deposed by them, and now he turnes a preacher under the devill of hellish doctrine. For the devill at this tyme preaches to his witches really (if I may so term it) the doctrine of the infernall pitt, viz., blasphemy against God and his son Christ.

Among other things, he told them that they were more happy in him than they could be in God. Him they saw, but God they could not see. And in mockrie of Christ and his holy ordinance of the sacrament of his supper, he gives the sacrament to them, bidding them eat it and to drink it in remembrance of himself. This villan was assisting to Sathan in this action and in preaching.
—ROBERT LAW, *Memorialls*, Edinburgh, 1818.

60. Elizabeth Gowdie's Horse and Hattock

Elizabeth Gowdie deposes: I haid a little horse, and wold say, "Horse and Hattock, in the Divellis name!" And then we wold flie away, quhair we wold, be ewin as strawes wold flie upon an hie-way. We will flie lyk strawes quhan we pleas; wild-strawes and corn-strawes wilbe horses to us, an we put thaim betwixt our foot and say, "Horse and Hattock in the Divellis name!" . . . Quhan we wold ryd, we tak windle-strawes or been-stakes and put them betwixt our foot, and say thryse:

"Horse and Hattok, horse and goe! Horse and pellatis, ho!" And immediatlie we flie away whair evir we wold . . . All the coeven did fflie lyk cattis, bot Barbara Ronald in Brightmanney and I, still read on an horse quhich we wold mak of a straw or a beein-stalk.*

—Criminal Trials

61. Ann Armstrong Ridden by Witches

Ann Armstrong (1673) saith that since she gave information against severall persons who ridd her to severall places where they had conversation with the divell, she hath been severall times lately ridden by Anne Driden and Anne Forster, and was last night ridden to the rideing house in the close on the common . . .

While she was lying in that condition (a fitt), which happened one night a little before Christmas, about the change of the moon, the informant see the said Anne Forster come with a bridle, and bridled her and ridd upon her crosse-legged till they came to the rest of her companions at Rideing Mill bridg-end where they usually mett. And when she light of her back (she) pulled the bridle of this informer's

---

*A hattock is a grain shock. Pellatis are presumably pallets, straw beds. Read: rode.

head, now in the likeness of the horse. But when the bridle was taken of, she stood up in her former shape . . .

Upon Cullop Monday last, being the tenth of February, the said persons met at Allensford, where this informant was ridden upon by an inchanted bridle by Michael Aynsley and Margaret his wife. Which inchanted bridle, when they tooke it from her head, she stood upp in her own proper person. . .

On Monday last at night, she being in her father's house, see one Jane Baites of Corbridge come in the forme of a gray catt with a bridle hanging on her foote, and breath'd upon her and struck her dead and bridled her, and rid upon her in the name of the devill southward, but the name of the place she does not now remember.

—*Surtees Society,* Vol. xl, Durham, 1861

62. The Devil in Wales

Sometime in the beginning of the last century, two old dames attended the morning service at Llandewi Brefi Church, and partook of the Holy Communion, but instead of eating the sacred bread like other communicants, they kept it in their mouths and went out. Then they walked round the church outside nine times, and at the ninth time the Evil One came out of the Church wall in the form of a frog, to whom they gave the bread from their mouths, and by doing this wicked thing they were supposed to be selling themselves to Satan and become witches. There was an old man in North Pembrokeshire, who used to say that he obtained the power of bewitching in the following manner: The bread of his first Communion he pocketed. He made pretence at eating it first of all, and then put it in his pocket. When he went out from the service there was a dog meeting him by the gate, to whom he gave the bread, thus selling his soul to the Devil. Ever after, he possessed the power to bewitch.

—J. Ceredig Davies, *Welsh Folklore,* Aberystwyth, 1911

* * *

Witchcraft or accusations of witchcraft were perhaps even more common in Scotland than they were south of the border. In this connection we shall hear more of Dr. John Fian in a moment, but before we come to the story of his plot against James VI it might be appropriate to set down a more amusing part of his long confession. It makes a small story quite worthy of Boccaccio.

63. John Fian's Love Magic Foiled

Fian had developed an overpowering passion for a young girl, the sister of one of his students. The said Doctor did also confesse that he had used meanes sundry times to obtaine his purpose and wicked intent of the same gentlewoman. And seeing himselfe disappointed of his intention, he determined by all wayes he might, to obtaine the same, trusting by conjuring witchcraft and sorcerie to obtaine it in this manner.

It happened this gentlewoman, being unmarried, had a brother who went to schoole with the said Doctor, and (he), calling the saide scholler to him, demaunded 'if he did lie with his sister,' who answered 'he did.' By meanes whereof hee thoughte to obtaine his purpose, and therefore secretly promised to teach him without stripes, so he would obtaine for him three hairs of his sisters privities at such (whatever) time as hee should spie out occasion for it. Which the youth promised faithfully to perform, and vowed speedily to put it in practise, taking a peece of conjured paper of his maister to lap them in when hee had gotten them.

And thereupon the boy practised nightly to obtaine his maisters purpose, especially when his sister was asleep. But God, who knoweth the secrets of all hearts and revealeth all wicked and ungodly practises would not suffer the intents of this divelish Doctor to come to that purpose which he supposed it would, and therefore, to declare that hee was heavily offended with his wicked intent, did so work by the gentlewoman's owne meanes that in the end the same was discovered and brought to light.

For shee, being one night asleepe, and her brother in bed with her, sodainly cried outt to her mother, declaring that her brother sould not suffer her to sleepe. Whereupon, her mother, having a quicke capacitie, did vehemently suspect Doctor Fian's intention, by reason she was a witch of her self, and therefore presently arose and was very inquisitive of the boy to understand his intent, and the better to know the same did beate him with sundrie stripes, whereby hee discovered the truth unto her.

The mother, therefore, being well practised in witchcraft, did thinke it most convenient to meete with the Doctor in his owne arte, and thereupon took the paper from the boy, wherein hee should have put the same haires, and went to a yong heyfer which never had borne calf, nor gone to the bull, and with a pair of sheeres clipped off three haires from the udder of the cow, and wrapt them in the same paper, which shee again delivered to the boy, then willing him to give the same to his saide maister, which he immediately did.

The schoole maister, so soone as he had received them, thinking them indeede to be the maid's haires, went straight and wrought his arte upon them. But the Doctor had no sooner doone his intent to them, but presently the hayfer cow, whose haires they were indeede, came unto the door of the church wherein the schoole maister was, into which the hayfer went and made towards the schoole maister, leaping and dauncing upon him and following him forth of the church and to what place soever he went, to the great admiration of all the townes men of Saltpans and many other who did beholde the same.

—Criminal Trials

* * *

In 1590 some thirty-nine people were arrested and charged with the attempted murder of James VI and his Queen by witchcraft. Barbara Napier, a lady of good family, Effie McCalyan, a daughter of Lord Cliftonhall, Agnes

Sampson or Simpson, a woman "grave and settled in her answers," and John Fian, a schoolmaster, seem to have been the leaders of the conspiracy, and their plan, if plan it was, strikes one as bizarre in the extreme.

First they tried with their incantations to raise a storm to wreck the Queen's ship on its way to Scotland. A storm did indeed rise, but it seems not to have been violent enough. Then, in the time-honored way of witches, they decided to mould and destroy wax effigies of their victims. If that did not work, they planned to use poison.

But the accused were not alone. They seem to have been plotting at the instigation of an individual far more important than they. Francis Stewart, Earl of Bothwell, would, if the King died without issue, have been next in line to the throne, not only of Scotland, but eventually of England too. And Barbara Napier (she was eventually acquitted) claimed as the motive for their crime "that another might have ruled in his Majesty's place, and the government might have gone to the Devil."

Agnes Simpson too confessed under torture that the wax images had been made at Bothwell's instigation. Then Dr. Fian was tortured and made a similar confession in the presence of the King.

That night, if one reads between the lines of the account, either Bothwell or one of his agents managed to slip into the prison and talk to him. That he in fact escaped on his own and without help seems unlikely in the extreme. He was of course in a desperate position. If he adhered to his confession (made in the hope of obtaining mercy) his companions would have him killed. If he retracted it he would be burned alive. So with Bothwell's help he escaped. His Devil-God (if we are to accept their worship of the devil at its face value) had snatched him out of the clutches of his enemies.

But the "devil" was not so much concerned with Fian's rescue as with undoing the damage he had caused. And having got clear, instead of being helped to flee the country, Dr. Fian was taken back to his own house. There, according to the King, he had a conversation with Bothwell. When he was at last recaptured he not only retracted his confession. He suffered further torture and death without allowing another word to pass his lips.

As for Bothwell, the "Devil" instigator, he shortly afterward fled the country and died at Naples in 1614. To print more than a small part of the proceedings would be to give them an importance out of all proportion. But interesting they are, if only because they deal, not with half-demented girls who are breathed on and "struck dead," bridled and ridden they know not where, but with ambitious and intelligent people who in the devil's name gambled for the highest stakes—and lost.

The first item, or at least one sentence of it, appears in an earlier excerpt (No. 57).

64. The Confession of Agnes Simpson

The Confession of Agnes Sympson to King James then of the Scots. . . . She confest before his Majesty that the Devil in Mans likeness met her going out in the Fields from her own House at Keith betwixt five and six at Even, being alone, and commandit her to be at Northberwick-Kirk the next night. And she past then on Horseback, conveyed by her good-son called John Couper, and lighted at the Kirk-yard or a little before she came to it, about eleven hours at Even.

They danced along the Kirk-yard. Geilie Duncan plaid to them on a Trump. John Fien (muffled?) led all the rest. The said Agnes and her Daughter followed next. Besides there were Kate Grey, George Moilis's wife, Robert Greirson, Katherine Duncan, Bessie Right, Isabel Gilmore, John Graymaill, Duncan Buchanan, Thomas Barnhil and his wife, Gilbert MacGil, Joh. Macgil, Katherine Macgil, with the rest of their complices above an hundred persons, whereof there were six Men, and all the rest Women.

The Women made first their homage, and then the Men. The Men were turned nine times widdershins about, and the Women six times. John Fien blew up the Doors and blew in the Lights, which were like mickle black Candles sticking round about the Pulpit. The Devil startit up himself in the Pulpit like a mickle black Man, and everyone answered *Here*.

Mr. Robert Greirson being named, they all ran hirdie girdie, and were angry: for it was promised he should be called Robert the Controller, alias Rob the Rowar . . .

The first thing he demandit was if they keept all promise and been good Servants, and what they had done since the last time they had convened. At his command they opened up three Graves, two within and one without the Kirk, and took off the Joints of their Fingers, toes and Neise, and parted them amongst them. And the said Agnes Sympson got for her part a Winding-sheet and two Joynts. The Devil commandit them to keep the Joynts upon them while they were dry, and to make a powder of them to do evil withal. Then he commandit them to keep his Commandments, which were to do all the evil they could. Before they departed they kiss'd his Breech. The Record speaks more broad, as I noted before. He had on him ane Gown and ane Hat, which were both black, and they that were assembled, part stood and part sate. John Fien was even nearest the Devil at his left Elbock. Graymaill keeped the door.

—JOSEPH GLANVILL, *Saducismus triumphatus*, London, 1689

65. The Confession of Agnes Thompson

Agnes Tompson confessed that at the time when his Majestie was in Denmarke, shee . . . took a cat and christened it, and afterward bound to each part of that cat the cheefest part of a dead man and severall joyntis of his bodie. And that in the night following the saide cat was conveyed into the middest of the sea by all these witches, sayling in their riddles or cives as aforesaid, and so left the saide cat right before the toune of Lieth in Scotland. This doone, there did arise such a tempest in the sea as a greater hath not been seene, which tempest was the cause of the perishing of a boat or vessell coming over from the towne of Brunt Ilande to the towne of Lieth, wherein were sundrie jewelles and rich giftes which should have been presented to the now Queene of Scotland at her Majesties coming to Lieth.

—*Criminal Trials*

66. The Torture and Death of John Fian

John Fian: after having been tortured he signed a confession in the presence of the King. Then he was by the maister of the prison committed to ward and appointed to a chamber by himselfe, where foresaking his wicked wayes, acknowledging his most ungodly lyfe, shewing that he had too much followed the allurements and enticements of Sathan and fondly practised his conclusions by conjuring, witchcraft, inchantment, sorcerie and such like, hee renounced the Devill and all his wicked workes, vowed to lead the lyfe of a Christian, and seemed newly converted to God.

The morrow after, upon conference with him, he granted that the Devill had appeared unto him in the night before appareled all in blacke with a white wande in his hande, and that the Devill demaunded of him "If hee woulde continue his faithfull service according to his first oath." Whome (as hee then saide) he utterly renounced to his face, and said unto him in this manner. "Avoide! Sathan, avoide! For I have listned too much unto thee, and by the same thou hast undone me. In respect whereof I utterly forsake thee." To whome the Devill answered that "once ere thou die, thou shalt bee mine." And with that (as he sayd) the Devill brake the white wand and immediately vanished foorth of his sight.

Thus all the daie this Doctor Fian continued verie solitarie, and seemed to have a care of his owne soul, and would call upon God, showing himselfe penitent for his wicked life. Nevertheless, the same night hee found such meanes that he stole the key of the prison doore and chamber in which he was, which in the night hee opened and fled awaie to the Saltpans where he was always resident and first apprehended.

Of whose sodaine departure, when the Kings Majestie had intelligence, hee presently commanded diligent inquirie to bee made for his apprehension. And for the better effecting thereof, he sent publicke proclamations into all partes of his lande to the same effect. By means of whose hot and harde pursuite he was agayn taken and brought to prison. And then, being called before the Kings Highnes, hee was re-examined, as well touching his departure as also touching all that had before happened.

But this Doctor, notwithstanding that his owne confession appeareth, remaining in recorde under his owne hande writting, and the same thereunto fixed in the presence of the Kings Majestie and the sundrie of his Councell, yet did hee utterly denie the same. Whereupon the Kings Majestie, perceiving his stubborne wilfulnesse, conceived and imagined that in the time of his absence hee had entered into newe conference and league with the Devill his maister. *(Fian was now again tortured in an effort to extract the truth.)* And notwithstanding all these grievous paines and cruel torments he would not confess anie thinges; so deeply had the Devill entered into his heart that he utterly denied all that which he before avouched, and would say nothing thereunto but this, that what he had done and sayde before was onely done and sayde for fear of paynes which he had endured.

So he was burned.

—*Criminal Trials*

67. The Death of Janet Cornfoot in Pittenweem

Of Janet Cornfoot, a suspected witch in Pittenweem (1704): Falling . . . into the hands of the populace, the wretched woman was tied hard up in a rope, beaten unmercifully, and then dragged by the heels through the streets and along the shore. The appearance of a Baillie for a brief space dispersed the crowd, but only to show how easily the authorities might have protected the victim if they had chosen. Resuming their

horrible work, the rabble tied Janet to a rope stretching between a vessel in the harbour and the shore, swinging her to and fro and amusing themselves by pelting her with stones. Tiring at length of this sport, they let her down with a sharp fall upon the beach, beat her again unmercifully, and finally covering her with a heavy door, pressed her to death.
—*Satan's Invisible World Discovered*

* * *

Though it has not strictly to do with witches, I feel I must include this further account from Sinclair, first because we all know the story, and second because it is interesting to see what the origin was of Browning's poem.

68. The Pied Piper of Hamelen

A Marvellous Prank plaid by the Devil at Hamelen, a town in Germany.

This City was annoyed with Rats and Mice. It happened that a Pied-Coated-Pyper came thither, who covenanted with the Chief Burgers for such a Reward if he should free them from the said Vermine, nor would he demand it till a twelve Moneth and a day after.

The Agreement being made, he began to play on his Pipes, and all the Rats and Mice followed him to a great Lough hard by, where they all perished; so the town was infected no more.

At the end of the year the Piper returned for his reward. The Burgers put him off with slighting and neglect, offering him some small matter which he refused. And staying some days in Town, on a Sunday morning at high Mass, when most People were at Church, he fell to play on his Pipes, and the Children up and down followed him out of the Town to a great hill not far off, which rent in two and opened, and let him and the Children in, and so closed up again.

This happened about two hundred and fifty years since. And in that Town they date their Bills and Bonds and other

Instruments in Law to this day from the year of this going out of their Children. Besides, there is a great pillar of stone erected at the foot of the said hill where this story is engraven.
—*Satan's Invisible World Discovered*

* * *

I think we cannot do better at this point than reintroduce a bit of Scot's mockery and common sense. He believed none of it, but at the same time, it was contemporaries of his who pressed the old woman to death in Pittenweem, and his American contemporaries (as we shall see in a moment) were suffering an outbreak of witch mania as great as any that had gone before.

69. Scot on Witches Confessions

If anie womans child chance to die at her hand so as no bodie knoweth how, it may not be thought or presumed that the mother killed it except she be supposed a witch. And in that case it is otherwise, for she must upon that presumption be executed . . .

Item, if the child of a woman that is suspected to be a witch be lacking or gone from hir, it is to be presumed that she hath sacrificed it to the divell, except she can proove the negative, or contrarie.

Item, though in other persons, certain points of their confessions may be thought erronious and imputed to error, yet in witches causes all oversights, imperfections and escapes must be judged impious and malicious, and tend to hir confusion and condemnation.

Item, though a theefe be not said in lawe to be infamous in any other matter than in theft, yet a witch defamed of witchcraft is said to be defiled with all manner of faults and infamies universalie . . . For rumors and reports are sufficient (saith Bodin) to condemne a witch.

Item, if any man, woman or child doo saie that such a one is a witch, it is a most vehement suspicion (saith Bodin) and sufficient to bring hir to the racke, though in all other cases it be directlie against lawe.

Item, in presumptions and suspicions against a witch, the common brute or voice of the people cannot erre.

Item, if a woman when she is apprehended crie out, or saie, "I am undone, save my life; I will tell you how the matter standeth;" &c., she is thereupon most vehementlie to be suspected and condemned to die.

Item, though a conjuror be not condemned for curing the diseased by vertue of his art, yet must a witch die for the like case.

Item, the behaviour, looks, becks and contenance of a woman are sufficient signes whereby to presume she is a witch. For alwaies they looke down to the ground, and dare not looke a man full in the face.

Item, , if their parents were thought to be witches, then it is certeinlie to be presumed that they are so, but it is not so to be thought of whoores.

Item, it is a vehement presumption if she cannot weepe at the time of hir examination, and yet Bodin saith that a witch may shed three drops out of hir right eie.

Item, it is not onelie a vehement suspicion and presumption, but an evident proofe of a witch if any man or beast die suddenlie where she hath beene seene latelie, though her witching stuffe be not found or espied.

Item, if any bodie use familiaritie or companie with a witch convicted, it is a sufficient presumption against that person to be adjudged a witch.

Item, that evidence that may serve to bring in any other person to examination may serve to bring a witch to her condemnation.

Item, herein judgement must be pronounced and executed (as Bodin saith) without order, and not like to an orderlie proceeding and forme of judgement in other crimes.

Item, a witch may not be brought to the torture suddenlie or before long examination, least she go awaie scot-free. For they feele no torments, and therefore care not for the same (as Bodin affirmeth).

Item, little children may be had to the torture at the first dash, but so may it not be doone with old women as is aforesaid.

Item, if she have anie privie marke under hir arm pokes, under hir haire, under hir lip or in her buttock or in hir privities, it is a presumption sufficient for the judge to proceed and give sentence of death upon hir.

The onelie pitie they shew to a poore woman in this case is that though she be accused to have slaine anie bodie with her inchantments, yet if she can bring foorth the partie alive, she shall not be put to death. Whereat I marvell, in as much as they can bring the divell in any bodies likenesse and representation.

Item, their lawe saith that an uncerteine presumption is sufficient when a certein presumption faileth.

—*Discoverie of Witchcraft,* IV. v

* * *

I think it very fitting to juxtapose the following with the diatribe of Scot just ended, for it demonstrates the truth of what he has to say better than a dozen arguments. With the exception of some last words spoken by the victims at Salem, it is, so far as I know, the only gallows dialogue with witches that has been preserved. The poor hags quite obviously hardly knew what they were saying, and the questions asked them, both by the clergyman and the sheriff are both sanctimonious and fatuous in the extreme.

70. A Gallows Dialogue with Three Witches

The Tryall, Condemnation and Execution of Three Witches, viz., Temperance Lloyd, Mary Lloyd and Susanna Edwards, Who were Arraigned at Exeter on the 18th of August, 1682. Also how they Confessed what Mischiefs they had done by the assistance of the Devil, who lay with the above-named Temperance Lloyd Nine Nights together; Also how they Squeezed one Hannah Thomas to death in their Arms; How they also caused several Ships to be cast away, causing a boy to fall from the top of a Main Mast into the sea. Printed for J. Deacon in Holborn, 1682.

* * *

> We must preface this account with a letter from Sir Francis North, First Baron Guilford and Lord Chancellor to Sir Leoline Jenkins, Secretary of State, cofounder of the Sheldonian theater and ex-Fellow of Jesus College, Oxford.

Here have been three old women condemned for witchcraft. Your curiosity will make you enquire of the circumstances. I shall only tell you what I had from my brother Raymond before whom they were tried, that they were the most old, decrepid, despicable, miserable creatures that ever he saw. A painter would have chosen them out of the whole country for figures of that kind to have drawn by. The evidence against them was very full and fanciful, but their confessions exceeded it. They appeared not only weary of their lives, but to have a great deal of skill to convict themselves. Their descriptions of the sucking devils with saucer-eyes were so natural that the jury could not choose but believe them. Sir, I find the country so fully possessed against them that, though some of the virtuosi may think these things the effects of confederacy, melancholy or delusion, and that young folks are altogether as quicksighted as they are old and infirm, yet we cannot reprieve them without appearing to deny the very being of witches, which, as it is contrary to law, so I think it would be ill for his Majesty's service, for it may give the faction occasion to set afoot the old trade of witch finding that may cost many innocent persons their lives, which this justice will prevent.

* * *

> Temperance, we read, went to her place of execution "eating all the way." Mary Trembles was "very obstinate and lay down." They had to tie her to her horse. A certain Reverend Mr. Hann tried, at the foot of the gallows, to elicit further information from them. His questions and their answers were taken down.

HANN: Mary Trembles, what have you to say as to the crime you are now to die for?

MARY: I have spoken as much as I can speak already, and can speak no more.

HANN: In what shape did the Devil come to you?

MARY: The Devil came to me once, I think, like a lion.

HANN: Did he offer any Violence to you?

MARY: No, not at all. But did frighten me, and did nothing to me. And I cried to God and asked what he would have, and he vanished.

HANN: Did he give thee any gift, or didst thou make him any promise?

MARY: No.

HANN: Had he any of thy blood?

MARY: No.

HANN: Did he come to make use of thy body in a carnal manner?

MARY: Never in my life.

HANN: Have you a teat in your private parts?

MARY: None.

HANN: Mary Trembles, was not the devil there with Susan when I was once in the prison with you, and under her coats? The other told me that he was there, but is now fled, and that the Devil was in the way when I was going to Taunton with my son, who is a minister. Thou speakest as a dying woman, and as the Psalmist says, "I will confess my iniquities and acknowledge all my sin." We find that Mary Magdalene had seven devils, and she came to Christ and obtained mercy. And if thou breakest thy league with the Devil and make a covenent with God, thou mayest also obtain mercy. If thou hast any thing to speak, speak thy mind.

MARY: I have spoken the very truth, and can speak no more. Mr. Hann, I would desire they may come by me and confess as I have done.

* * *

HANN: Temperance Lloyd, have you made any contract with the devil?

TEMPERANCE: No.

HANN: Did he ever take any of thy blood?

TEMP: No.
HANN: How did he appear to thee first? Or where? In the street? In what shape?
TEMP: In a woeful shape.
HANN: Did he ever have any carnal knowledge of thee?
TEMP: No. Never.
HANN: What did he do when he came to thee?
TEMP: He caused me to go and do harm.
HANN: And did you go?
TEMP: I did hurt a woman sore against my conscience. He carried me up to her door, which was open. The woman's name was Mrs. Grace Thomas.
HANN: What caused you to do her harm? What malice had you against her? Did she do you any harm?
TEMP: No, she never did me any harm. But the Devil beat me about the head grievously because I would not kill her. But I did bruise her after this fashion *(laying her two hands to her sides.)*
HANN: Did you bruise her till the blood came out of her mouth and nose?
TEMP: No.
HANN: How many did you destroy and hurt?
TEMP: None but she.
HANN: Did you know any mariners that you or your associates destroyed by overturning of ships and boats?
TEMP: No. I never hurt any ship, bark or boat in my life.
HANN: Was it you or Susan that did bewitch the children?
TEMP: I sold apples, and the child took an apple from me. And the mother took the apple from the child, for which I was very angry. But the child died of the small pox.
HANN: Did you know one Mr. Lutteril about these parts, or any of your confederates?
TEMP: No.
HANN: Temperance, how did you come in to hurt Mrs. Grace Thomas? Did you pass through the key-hole of the door, or was the door open?
TEMP: The Devil did lead me up stairs, and the door was open, and this is all the hurt I did.
HANN: How did you know it was the Devil?
TEMP: I knew it by his eyes.
HANN: Had you no discourse or treaty with him?

TEMP: No. He said I should go along to destroy a woman, and I told him I would not. He said he would make me. And then the Devil beat me about the head.
HANN: Why had you not called upon God?
TEMP: He would not let me do it.
HANN: You say you never hurt ships or boats. Did you never ride over an arm of the sea on a cow?
TEMP: No. No, Master, 'twas she *(meaning Susan.)*

When Temperance said 'twas Susan, she said she lied, and that she was the cause of bringing her to die, for she said when she first (was) brought to gaol, if that she was hanged, she would have me hanged too. She reported I should ride on a cow before her, which I never did.

HANN: Susan, did you see the shape of a bullock? At the first time of your examination, you said it was like a short black man about the length of your arm.
SUSAN: He was black, Sir.
HANN: Susan, had you any knowledge of the bewitching of Mr. Lutteril's child? Or did you know a place called Tranton Burroughs?
SUSAN: No.
HANN: Are you willing to have any prayers?

Then Mr. Hann prayed, whose prayer we could not take, and they sung part of the 40th Psalm at the desire of Susanna Edwards. As she mounted the ladder, she said, "The Lord Jesus speed me. Though my sins be red as scarlet, the Lord can make them as white as snow. The Lord help my soul. Lord Jesus speed me." Then was executed.

Mary Trembles said, "Jesus receive my soul. Lord Jesus speed me." Then was executed.

Temperance Lloyd said, "Jesus Christ speed me well. Lord, forgive all my sins. Lord Jesus, be merciful to my poor soul."

MR. SHERIFF: You are looked on as the woman that has debauched the other two. Did you ever lie with the Devil?
TEMP: No.
SHER: Did you not know of their coming to gaol?
TEMP: No.
SHER: Have you anything to say to satisfy the world?
TEMP: I forgive them as I desire the Lord Jesus Christ

will forgive me. The greatest thing I did was to Mrs. Grace Thomas, and I desire I may be sensible of it, and that the Lord Jesus Christ may forgive me. The Devil met me in the street and bid me kill her. And because I would not, he beat me about the head and back.

SHER: In what shape or colour was he?
TEMP: In black, like a bullock.
SHER: How do you know you did it? How went you in, through the key-hole or the door?
TEMP: At the door.
SHER: Had you no discourse with the devil?
TEMP: Never but this day six weeks.
SHER: You were charged about twelve years since, and did you never see the Devil but this time?
TEMP: Yes, once before. I was going for brooms, and he came to me and said, "This poor woman has a great burthen," and would ease me of my burthen, and I said, "The Lord has enabled me to carry it so far, and I hope I shall be able to carry it further."
SHER: Did the Devil never promise you any thing?
TEMP: No, never.
SHER: Then you have served a very bad Master, who gave you nothing. Well, consider you are just departing this world. Do you believe there is a God?
TEMP: Yes.
SHER: Do you believe in Jesus Christ?
TEMP: Yes. And I pray Jesus Christ to pardon all my sins.
And so was executed.

71. The Eyebiting Witches of Ireland

The Irishmen addict themselves wonderfullie to the credit and practice hereof. Insomuch as they affirme that not onelie their children, but their cattell are (as they call it) eybitten when they fall suddenly sicke, and terme one sort of their witches eybiters, onelie in that respect. Yea, and they will not sticke to affirme that they can rime either man or beast to death. Also the West Indians and Muscovites doo the like. And the Hunnes (as Gregory Turonensis writeth) used the helpe of witches in time of war.

—*Discoverie of Witchcraft,* III. xv

* * *

But Scot could be more than witty or argumentative. He could also tell a story that made his point perfectly clear.

72. Simon Davie's Bewitched Wife

But that it may appeere that even voluntarie confession (in this case) may be untrulie made, though it tend to the destruction of the confessor, and that melancholie may moove imaginations to that effect, I will cite a notable instance concerning this matter, the parties themselves being yet alive and dwelling in the parish of Sellenge* in Kent, and the matter not long sithence in this sort performed.

One Ade Davie, the wife of Simon Davie, husbandman, being reputed a right honest bodye, and being of good parentage, grew suddenlie (as hir husband informed me, and as is well knowne in these parts) to be somewhat pensive and more sad than in times past. Which thing, though it greeved him, yet he was lothe to make it so appeere as either his wife might be troubled or discontented therewith, or his neighbours informed thereof (least ill husbandrie should be laid to his charge, which in these quarters is much abhorred).

But when she grew from pensiveness to some perturbation of mind, so as hir accustomed rest began in the night season to be withdrawne from hir through sighing and secret lamentation, and that, not without teares, hee could not but demand the cause of hir conceipt and extraordinarie moorning. But although at that time she covered the same,

---
*Modern Sellindge, just north of the Romney Marsh.

acknowledging nothing to be amisse with hir, soone after notwithstanding, she fell downe before him on hir knees, desiring him to forgive hir, for she had greevouslye offended (as she said) God and him.

Hir poore husband, being abashed at this hir behaviour, comforted hir as he could, asking hir the cause of hir trouble and greefe. Who told him that she had (contrarie to God's lawe) and to the offense of all good Christians, to the injurie of him, and speciallie to the losse of hir owne soule, bargained and given hir soule to the divell to be delivered unto him within short space.

Whereunto hir husband answered, saieng, "Wife, be of good cheere. This thy bargaine is void and of none effect. For thou hast sold that which is none of thine to sell, sith it belongeth to Christ, who hath bought it and deerely paid for it, even with his bloud which he shed upon the crosse." So as the divell hath no interest in thee.

After this, with like submission, teares and penitence, she said unto him, "Oh, husband, I have yet committed another fault and doone you more injurie. For I have bewitched you and your children."

"Be content" (quoth he), "by the grace of God, Jesus Christ shall unwitch us, for none evill can happen to them that feare God."

And (as trulie as the Lord liveth) this was the tenor of his words unto me, which I knowe is true, as proceeding from unfeigned lips, and from one that feareth God. Now when the time approched that the divell should come and take possession of the woman according to his bargaine, he watched and praied earnestlie, and caused his wife to read psalmes and praiers for mercie at Gods hands. And suddenlle about midnight there was a great rumbling belowe under his chamber window, which amazed them exceedingly. For they conceived that the divell was beelowe, though he had no power to come up because of their fervent prayers.

He that noteth this womans first and second confession, freelie and voluntarilie made, how everie thing concurred that might serve to adde credit thereunto and yeeld matter for hir condemnation, would not thinke but that if Bodin were foreman of hir inquest, he would crie: "Guiltie!" and would hasten execution upon hir, who would have said as much before any judge in the world, if she had been examined, and have confessed no lesse if she had been arraigned thereupon.

But God knoweth she was innocent of anie these crimes, howbeit she was brought lowe and pressed downe with the weight of this humor, so as both hir rest and sleepe were taken awaie from hir, and hir fansies troubled and disquieted with despaire, and other such cogitations as grew by occasion thereof.

And yet I beleeve, if any mishap had insued to hir husband or hir children, few witchmongers would have judged otherwise but that she had bewitched them. And she (for hir part) so constantlie persuaded hirselfe to be a witch that she judged hir selfe worthie of death. Insomuch as, being reteined in hir chamber, she sawe not anie one carriend a faggot to the fier but she would saie it was to make a fier to burne hir for her witchirie. But God knoweth she had bewitched none, neither insued there anie hurt unto anie by hir imagination, but unto hir selfe.

And as for the rumbling, it was by occasion of a sheepe which was flawed and hoong by the wals, so as a dog came and devoured it. Whereby grew the noise which I before mentioned. And she being now recovered, remaineth a right honest woman.

—*Discoverie of Witchcraft*, III. x

* * *

What are witches supposed to be able to do, Scot asks, and in one small swoop he plunders the authorities to come up with an answer.

73. Scot on Witchcraft as Superstition

Ovid affirmeth that they can raise and suppresse lightening and thunder, raine and haile, clouds and winds, tempests and earthquakes. Others doo write that they can pull down the moone and starres. Some write that with wishing they can send needles into the livers of their enemies. Some that they can transferre corne in the blade from one place to another. Some, that they can cure diseases supernaturallie, flie in the aire and danse with divels. Some write that they can plaie the part of Succubus and contract themselves to Incubus, and so yoong prophets are upon them begotten, &c.

Some saie they can transsubstantiate themselves and others, and take the forms and shapes of asses, woolves, ferrets, cowes, apes, horsses, dogs, &c. Some say they can keepe divels and spirits in the likenesse of todes and cats.

They can raise spirits (as others affirme), drie up springs, turne the course of running water, inhibit the sunne and staie both day and night, changing the one into the other. They can go in and out at awger holes, and saile in an egg shell, a cockle or muscle shell, through and under the tempestuous seas. They can go invisible and deprive men of their privities, and otherwise of the act and use of venerie. They can bring soules out of the graves. They can teare snakes in peeces with words, and with looks kill lambes. But in this case a man may saie that *miranda canunt sed non credendo poetae*. They can also bring to passe that chearne as long as you list, your butter will not come, especiallie if either the maids have eaten up the creame or the goodwife have sold the butter before in the market. Whereof I have had some triall, although there may be true and naturalll causes to hinder the common course thereof. As for example, put a little sope or sugar into your chearne of creame and there will never come anie butter, chearne as long as you list.

But *Malleus Maleficarum* saith that there is not so little a village where manie women are not that bewitch, infect and kill kine and dry up the milk, alledging for the strengthening of that assertion the saieng of the Apostle, *Nunquid Deo cura est de bobus?* Doth God take anie care of oxen?

—*Discoverie of Witchcraft*, I. iv

74. Death for Witchcraft in Angola

I was at Mabrizette when three Cabinda women had been to the river with their pots for water. All three were filling them from the stream together when the middle one was snapped up by an alligator and instantly carried away under the surface of the water, and of course drowned. The relatives of the poor woman at once accused the other two of bewitching her and causing the alligator to take her out of their midst. When I remonstrated with them, and attempted to show them the utter absurdity of the charge, their answer was: "Why did not the alligator take one of the end ones then, and not the one in the middle?" And out of this idea it was impossible to move them, and the poor women were both obliged to take *casca* (a deadly poison). I never heard the result, but most likely one or both were either killed or passed into slavery.

—J. J. MONTEIRO, *Angola and the River Congo*, 1875

75. Witchcraft in Papua

Maudega, a woman of Avetan in Murua, had been on a visit to the neighbouring village of Nabudau, and on her return had brought back with her the daughter of Boiamai, the Nabudau chief. The child was unfortunately taken by a crocodile, and in revenge Boiamai, with his son and some other men of the village, killed Maudega and three of her relations . . . At the trial the son made the following statement. "It is true we killed these people . . . Maudega took my sister away to her village, and while she was there she bewitched an alligator and made it come out of the water and take away my sister and eat her.

—J. H. P. MURRAY, *Papua*, 1912

76. The Basuto Ordeal by Boiling Water

Yesterday morning a (Basuto) woman from a nearby village came to let me know that she was about to go through the ordeal of boiling water because she had been accused of being a witch. A close neighbour who was a very wicked woman had plagued her for months, and was always telling people that she was a witch. So at last she had decided to subject herself to the ordeal by water (one plunged one's hands into boiling water). She was not at all afraid of the test she was to undergo, for she knew herself to be innocent, and was certain that the water would not burn her.

—*Missions evangeliques*, lxxxi
'Th. Burnier

77. A Scapegoat Among the A-Kamba

Among the Kitui section certain persons are found who are believed to be congenitally unclean and bearers of ill luck; if such a person counted people or live-stock he would by thus doing bestow ill-fortune, and the people or stock would probably sicken or die. They state they have no reason for suspecting a person beforehand, but if any untoward sickness occurs they are often apt to pitch upon someone as a scapegoat. The accused is called up and requested to spit upon the sick person or beast; it is believed that this will exorcise the curse.

—C. W. HOBLEY, *Ethnology of the A-Kamba*

78. A Man and His Wife Murdered for Witchcraft

A man and his wife in the immediate neighbourhood of Mount Coke (Kaffraria) were deliberately and in cold blood murdered by the man's brother on a charge of witchcraft. Early in the morning one of the victims was called from his own residence by his brother who, with a party of five others, was waiting his arrival. The moment he entered the door a thong was cast about his neck; he was dragged for some distance and beaten to death with sticks. The party then proceeded to the garden of the deceased, where his wife was found, who suffered a similar fate. The house was then burnt, the only child of the deceased (a daughter) carried off and the cattle driven to the kraal of the murderer.

—*Wesleyan Missionary Notices*, iv
(Letter from Reverend W. Impey)

79. The Bewitching of John Tonken

Cornwall Summer Sessions and Gaol Delivery holden at Launceston on 27 July:

One John Tonken of Pensans near the Mount in Cornwall, about fifteen or sixteen years of age was in April last strangely taken with sudden fits; and on the 4th of May, 1686 as he lay in bed, there appeared to him a woman in a blue jerkin and red petticoat with yellow and green patches, and told him that he would not be well before he had brought up nut-shells, pins and nails; which the boy afterwards related to several people that were at his chamber, though none did hear or see the apparition but himself; soon after, the lad was taken with fits of striving or yoaking, insomuch that two men could scarce hold him, and after several fits he brought up three pins and half a walnut-shell, and in a few days after he brought up three walnut-shells and several pins, some of which were crooked. The woman very often appeared to

Still as the Witch was ready to reply, he would cross her with one scurvy jest, and betwen every jest drink to her, yet him, sometimes in the shape as before, at other times like a cat; whereupon the boy would shriek and cry out that he would not see her, laying his hands over his eyes and mouth, and would say with a loud voice, "She is putting things in my mouth. She will choke me. She will poison me." At other times he would say, "I will not be tempted by thee, and in the name of Jesus, I defy thee and all thy works." For a while he would lie as dead, and on a sudden he would spring from the bed three or four feet high from between two men that actually sat upon the bed by him.

Then there appeared three women, wherat he cried out, "What a confederacy! What, you old witch, more confederates?" And then she bad him farewell and said she would trouble him no more. And two days after the boy was pretty well again, and goes abroad with crutches. One Jane Nicholas was indicted and tried, but found not guilty.

—*A True Account of a Strange and Wonderful Relation of one John Tonken of Pensans in Cornwall,* London, 1686

80. A Drunkard Bewitched in Royston

There was an honest fellow, and as boon a companion dwelling in Royston, one that loved the pot with the long neck almost as well as his prayers; for (quoth he) as I know one is medicinable for the soul, I am sure the other's physic for the body. It was this Fuddle-cap's chance with three or four as good malt-worms as himself, and as sure, where the best lap was to be found, together as four knaves in a 'payre of cards', to be drinking where this Witch came in and stood 'gloting upon them.'

Now this good fellow (not enduring to look upon a bad face but his own, especially when he is cup-shot) called aloud to her, "Do you hear, Witch, look tother ways. I cannot abide a nose of that fashion, or else turn your face the wrong side outward. It may look like raw flesh for flies to blow maggots in."

swear, "God damn him, she should starve ere she should have a drop on't. Her breath's so strong and would so stick in the cup that all the water that runs by Ware would not wash it out again."

At last the Witch got so much time to call to him, "Dost thou hear, good friend? (quoth she), "that thou throwest in they drink apace, but shall not find it so easy coming out."

"Nay, as for coming out" (answered the fellow), "I throwed it in above, and it shall come out beneath, and then thou shalt have some of it if thou wilt, because I am in hope it will poison thee."

Then with this greeting, away goes the Witch in a chafe and the fellow sits down to follow his drink. But as the end of all drunkards is either to ming* or to sleepe, so out goes this fellow, and drawing his Gentleman usher against a pale side, finds me a top of his nose a red lump as big as a cherry, and in his belly felt such a rumbling as if the Tower of Babel had fallen about his ears.

Oh, the sight thereof draws his heart to an ague and his tongue to an alarum, and out he cries, "The Witch, the Witch, I am undone, I am undone! O God, women of Royston, help, help, the Witch, the Witch. I am a man spoiled. Help, I am undone."

At that word help, the Witch, in comes one of his fellows running in haste, and asked him, what, should they help the Witch? "Oh," (quoth he) "to the gallows, for I am undone by her."

Well, yet out he runs where for that night she would not be found, but the next morning meeting her in a lane, his pain rather increased than lessened, and there feasts his ten commandments upon her. He almost scratched out her eyes, nay, left her not till he brought her to the town, where for this and the rest she was apprehended, and she and her daughter, with George Dell and his mother, worthily suffered death the 4th of August.

—*The Most Cruell and Bloody Murder committed by an Inkeeper's Wife called Annis Dell* . . .
London, 1606 (Printed in Ewen,
C. L'Estrange, *Witchcraft and Demonianism*, London, 1933.)

---

*To ming is to remember. Presumably, in this case, to indulge in reminiscence.

81. Twelve African Woman Accused of Witchcraft

In 1876 an Akale chief, Kasa, was charged by an elephant he had wounded, and was pierced by its tusks. His attendants drove off the beast; the fearfully lacerated man survived long enough to accuse twelve of his women and other slaves of having bewitched his gun, thus causing it only to wound, instead of killing the elephant.
—R. H. NASSAU, *Fetichism in West Africa*, 1904

* * *

It would be good to follow Scot's mockery and the "roystering" in Royston with the very different and sometimes frightening evidence out of Salem. Salem documents are frightening because they reveal as no other documents do the irrational at its work of destroying simple people. They show us the faces of both victims and persecutors plain.

But in the interests of chronological order, I think Salem must wait until last, because it was of course the last major outbreak of this particular madness in the Western world.

So before that, Glanvill and certain extracts from his Saducismus triumphatus, *posthumously published in 1681. I have used the fourth edition in this work. It appeared in 1689. Joseph Glanvill (1636–1680) came down from Exeter College, Oxford, to write on nonconformists (he was against them), to be elected one of the original Fellows of the Royal Society, to be made Chaplain to Charles II, and to end his life as rector of the Abbey Church in Bath. He has been called, not unjustly, the father of modern psychical research.*

His collection of twenty-six "relations" has never been equalled as a compilation of the purely evidential. In spite of being a theologian, and in spite of being, like most of his contemporaries, a moderately superstitious man, he wanted above all to discover precisely what happened. And many of his stories are simply records of hearings before his friend, Robert Hunt, a Somerset magistrate. But even in the accounts he compiles from other sources, he is perpetually anxious to remain logical, to examine the accuracy and veracity of witnesses, and to leave as little room as possible for the fanciful or purely speculative.

The result, of course, is that first of all he compiled good, solid stories, full of a sense for both character and the dramatic. If his witnesses sometimes seem to us a little credulous, if their sense for method looks to our eyes to be mixed with an ingenuous readiness to believe, there is in Glanvill at least an attempt to avoid doctrinaire solutions.

His informants put down what they saw, listened to what both victim and victimizer said. They tried hard to be just, and Glanvill himself desired to use only what was "modern" and well attested.

The story of the drummer of Tedworth is probably as memorable and as nearly immortal as such a story can be. The witches of Blokula are familiar to all specialists in the subject. Jane Brooks' fate has always seemed to me particularly moving. In a word, the stories are complete in themselves (thus longer than the ones I have so far used). They were investigated and written down just when a real attempt was being made for the first time to examine such phenomena with something approaching scientific precision. And they are good stories, all of them. That alone justifies their inclusion in this book.

82. Jane Brooks Hanged for Witchcraft

On Sunday, the 15. of November, 1657, about Three of the Clock in the Afternoon, Richard Jones, then a sprightly youth about twelve years old, Son of Henry Jones of Shepton Mallet in the County of Somerset, being in his Father's House alone, and perceiving one looking in at the Windows, went to the door, where one Jane Brooks of the same Town (but then by name unknown to this Boy) came to him.

She desired him to give her a piece of close Bread, and gave him an Apple. After which she also stroked him down on the right side, shook him by the hand, and so bid him good night. The youth returned into the House, where he had been left well when his Father and one Gibson went from him, but at their return, which was in an hour or thereabout, they found him ill and complaining of his right side, in which the pain continued the most part of that night.

And on Munday following in the Evening the Boy rosted the Apple he had of Jane Brooks, and having eaten about half of it, was extreamly ill and sometimes speechless, but being recovered, he told his Father that a Woman of the Town on Sunday before had given him that Apple, and that she stroked him on the side. He said he knew not her name, but should her person if he saw her.

Upon this, Jones was advised to invite the Women of Shipton to come to his House upon the occasion of his Sons illness, and the Child told him that in case the Woman should come in when he was in his Fit, if he were not able to speak he would give him an intimation by a Jogg, and desired that his Father would then lead him through the Room, for he said he would put his hand upon her if she were there. After this, he continuing very ill, many Women came daily to see him. And Jane Brooks the Sunday after came in with two of her Sisters, and several other Women of the Neighbourhood were there.

Upon her coming in, the Boy was taken so ill that for some time he could not see or speak, but having recovered his sight, he gave his father the Item, and he led him about the Room. The boy drew towards Jane Brooks who was behind her two Sisters and the other Women, and put his hand upon her, which, his Father perceiving, immediately scratcheth her Face and drew Blood from her. The Youth then presently cryed out that he was well, and so he continued seven or eight days.

But then, meeting with Alice Coward, Sister to Jane Brooks, who passing by, said to him, "How do you, my Honey?" he presently fell ill again. And after that the said Coward and Brooks often appeared to him. The Boy would describe the Cloths and Habit they were in at the time exactly, as the Constable and others have found upon repairing to them, though Brooks's House was at a good distance from Jones's. This they often tried, and always found the Boy right in his Descriptions.

On a certain Sunday about Noon, the Child being in a

Room with his Father and one Gibson, and in his Fit, he on the sudden called out that he saw Jane Brooks on the Wall, and pointed to the place, where immediately Gibson struck with a Knife. Upon which the Boy cryed out, "O Father, cooz Gibson hath cut Jane Brooks' hand and 'tis Bloody."

The Father and Gibson immediately repaired to the Constable, a discreet Person, and acquainting him with what had passed, desired him to go with them to Jane Brook's House, which he did. They found her sitting in her Room on a Stool with one hand over the other.

The Constable askt her how she did. She answered, not well. He askt again why she sat with one hand over the other. She replied she was wont to do so. He enquired if anything were amiss with her Hand. Her answer was it was well enough. The Constable desired he might see the Hand that was under, which she being unwilling to shew him, he drew it out and found it bloody, according to what the Boy had said. Being askt how it came so, she said 'twas scratched with a great Pin.

On the Eighth of December, 1657, the Boy, Jane Brooks and Alice Coward appeared at Castle-Cary before the Justices, Mr. Hunt and Mr. Cary. The Boy having begun to give his Testimony, upon the coming in of the two Women and their looking on him, was instantly taken Speechless, and so remained till the Women were removed out of the Room. And then in a short time, upon Examination, he gave a full relation of the mentioned particulars.

On the Eleventh of January following, the Boy was again examined by the same Justices at Shepton Mallet, and upon the sight of Jane Brooks was again taken Speechless, but was not so afterwards when Alice Coward came into the Room to him.

On the next appearance at Shepton, which was on the Seventeenth of February, there were present many Gentlemen, Ministers and others. The Boy fell into his Fit upon the sight of Jane Brooks, and lay in a Man's Arms like a dead Person. The Woman was then willed to lay her Hand on him, which she did, and he thereupon started and sprang out in a very strange and unusual manner.

One of the Justices, to prevent all possibilities of

Legerdemain, caused Gibson and the rest to stand off from the Boy, and then that Justice himself held him, the Youth being blindfolded. The Justice called as if Brooks should touch him, but winked to others to do it, which two or three successively did, but the Boy appeared not concerned. The Justice then called on the Father to take him, but had privately before desired one Mr. Geoffrey Strode to bring Jane Brooks to touch him at such a time as he should call for his Father, which was done, and the Boy immediately sprang out after a very odd and violent fashion. He was after touched by several Persons and moved not, but Jane Brooks being again caused to put her Hand upon him, he started and sprang out twice or thrice as before. All this while he remained in his Fit, and some time after. And being then laid on a Bed in the same Room, the People present could not for a long time bow either of his Arms or Legs.

Between the mentioned 15 of November and the 11 of January the two Women appeared often to the Boy, their Hands cold, their Eyes staring, and their Lips and Cheeks looking pale. In this manner on a Thursday about Noon, the Boy being newly laid into his Bed, Jane Brooks and Alice Coward appeared to him, and told him that what they had begun they could not perform. But if he would say no more of it they would give him Money, and so put a Two-pence into his Pocket. After which they took him out of his Bed, laid him on the ground and vanished, and the Boy was found by those that came next into the Room, lying on the Floor as if he had been dead. The Two-pence was seen by many, and when it was put into the Fire and hot, the Boy would fall ill. But as soon as it was taken out and cold, he would be again as well as before. This was seen and observed by a Minister, a discreet Person when the Boy was in one Room and the Two-pence (without his knowledge) put into the Fire in another, and this was divers times tried in the presence of several Persons.

Between the 8 of December and the 17 of February in the Year mentioned, divers Persons at sundry times heard in the Boy a noise like the croaking of a Toad, and a voice within him saying "Jane Brooks, Alice Coward," twelve times in near a quarter of an hour. At the same time some held a

Candle before the Boys Face, and earnestly looked on him, but could not perceive the least motion of his Tongue, Teeth or Lips while the Voice was heard.

On the 25 of February between two and three in the Afternoon, the Boy being at the House of Richard Isles in Shepton Mallet, went out of the Room into the Garden. Isles, his Wife followed him, and was within two Yards when she saw him rise up from the ground before her, and so mounted higher and higher till he passed in the Air over the Garden-Wall, and was carried so above ground more than thirty Yards, falling at last at one Jordan's Door at Shepton, where he was found as dead for a time. But coming to himself, told Jordan that Jane Brooks had taken him up by the Arm out of Isles his Garden, and carried him in the Air as is related.

The Boy at several other times was gone on the sudden, and upon a search after him found in another Room as dead, and at some times strangely hanging above the ground, his Hands being flat against a great Beam in the top of the Room, and all his Body two or three Foot from ground. There he hath hung a quarter of an hour together, and being afterwards come to himselfe, he told those that found him that Jane Brooks had carried him to that place and held him there. Nine People at a time saw the Boy so strangely hanging by the Beam.

From the 15 of November to the 10 of March following, he was by reason of his Fits much wasted in his body and unspirited, but after that time, being the day the two Women were sent to Gaol, he had no more of these Fits. Jane Brooks was Condemned and Executed at Charde Assizes, March 26, 1658.

This is the sum of Mr. Hunts Narrative, which concludes with both the Justices attestation, thus:

The aforesaid passages were some of them seen by us; and the rest, and some other remarkable ones not here set down were upon the Examination of several creditable Witnesses taken upon Oath before us.

Subscribed,
Rob. Hunt, John Cary

—Saducismus triumphatus

* * *

Ann Putnam and many other children at Salem seem to have suffered the same "fits" at the instigation of people they thought of as witches. So far as one can judge, the "fits" were quite genuine and were hysterical in origin. Such hysterical attacks seem generally to have ceased at the beginning of puberty.

83. Julian Cox and Her Toad

. . . Another Witness swore that as he passed by Cox her Door, she was taking a Pipe of Tobacco upon the Threshold of her Door, and invited him to come in and take a Pipe, which he did. And as he was taking, Julian (Cox) said to him, "Neighbour, look what a pretty thing there is." He looked down, and there was a Monstrous great Toad betwixt his Leggs, staring him in the face. He endeavoured to kill it by spurning it, but could not hit it. Whereupon Julian bad him forbear, and it would do him no hurt. But he threw down his Pipe and went home (which was about two Miles off Julian Cox her House) and told his Family what had happened, and that he believed it was one of Julian Cox her Devils. After, he was taking a Pipe of Tobacco at home, and the same Toad appeared betwixt his Leggs. He took the Toad out to kill it, and to his thinking cut it in several pieces, but returning to his Pipe, the Toad still appeared. He endeavoured to burn it, but could not. At length he took a Switch and beat it. The Toad ran several times about the Room to avoid him, he still pursuing it with correction. At length the Toad cryed and vanished, and he was never after troubled with it.

—*Saducismus triumphatus*

84. A Maori Lizard in the Path

If a traveller should see a lizard in the path before him, he would know the creature had not come there of its own accord, but had been sent by an enemy as an *aitua* (evil omen) to cause his death. He therefore at once kills the reptile, and craves a woman to step over it as it lies in the path. By this means the evil omen is averted.

—W. H. GOLDIE, *Maori Medical Lore*
(*Transactions* of the New Zealand Institute), 1904

85. *Atua* in New Zealand

A native (New Zealand) came to me, apparently in deep decline. He had caught cold, and had not taken care of himself. The natives are not in the least aware of the causes of their diseases. They ascribe to *Atua* everything that gives them pain. The deluded man said *Atua* was within him, eating his vitals.

—*Missionary Register*, August, 1917

86. The Drummer of Tedworth

Mr. John Mompesson of Tedworth in the County of Wilts, being about the middle of March in the year 1661 at a Neighboring Town called Ludgershall, and hearing a Drum beat there, he inquired of the Bailiff of the Town, at whose House he then was, what it meant.

The Bailiff told him that they had for some days been troubled with an idle Drummer who demanded Money of the Constable by vertue of a pretended Pass, which he thought was counterfeit.

Upon this, Mr. Mompesson sent for the Fellow, and askt him by what Authority he went up and down the Country in that manner with his Drum. The Drummer answered he had good authority, and produced his Pass, with a Warrant under the Hands of Sir William Cawle and Colonel Ailiff of Grevenham. Mr. Mompesson, knowing these Gentlemens Hands, discovered that the Pass and Warrant were counterfeit, and thereupon commanded the Vagrant to put off his Drum, and charged the Constable to carry him before the next Justice of the Peace to be further examined and punisht. The Fellow then confessed the Cheat, and begged earnestly to have his Drum. Mr. Mompesson told him that if he understood from Colonel Ailiff, whose Drummer he said he was, that he had been an honest Man, he should have it again, but in the meantime he would secure it. So he left the Drum with the Bailiff and the Drummer in the Constable's hands, who it seems was prevailed on by the Fellows intreaties to let him go.

About the middle of April following, when Mr. Mompesson was preparing for a Journey to London, the Bailiff sent the Drum to his House. When he was returned from that Journey his Wife told him that they had been much affrighted in the Night by Thieves, and that the House had been like to have been broken up. And he had not been at home above three Nights when the same noise was heard that had disturbed his Family in his absence. It was a very great knocking at his Doors and the outsides of his House. Hereupon he got up and went about the House with a Brace of Pistols in his hands. He opened the Door where the great knocking was, and then he heard the noise at another Door. He opened that also, and went out round his House, but could discover nothing, only he still heard a strange noise and hollow sound. When he got back to Bed the noise was Thumping and Drumming on the top of his House, which continued a good space and then by degrees went off into the Air.

After this the noise of Thumping and Drumming was very frequent, usually five Nights together, and then it would intermit three. It was on the outsides of the House, which is most of it of Board. It constantly came as they were going to sleep, whether early or late. After a months disturbance without, it came into the Room where the Drum lay four or five nights in seven within half an hour after they were in Bed, continuing almost two. The sign of it just before it came was, they still heard an hurling in the Air over the House, and at its going off the beating of a Drum, like that at the breaking up of a Guard. It continued in this Room for the space of two Months, which time Mr. Mompesson himself lay there to observe it. In the fore part of the night it used to be very troublesome, but after two hours all would be quiet.

Mrs. Mompesson being brought to bed, there was but little noise the night she was in Travail, nor any for three Weeks after till she had recovered strength. But after this civil cessation it returned in a ruder manner than before, and followed and vexed the youngest Children, beating their Bedsteads with that violence that all present expected they would fall in pieces. In laying Hands on them, one should feel no blows, but micht perceive them to shake exceedingly. For an Hour together it would beat Round-heads and Cuckolds, the Tat-too and several other points of War as well as any Drummer. After this they should hear a scratching under the Childrens Bed as if by something that had Iron Tallons. It would lift the Children up in their Beds, follow them from one Room to another, and for a while haunted none particularly but them.

There was a Cock-loft in the House which had not been observed to be troubled. Thither they removed the Children, putting them to Bed while it was fair day, where they were no sooner laid, but their troubler was with them as before.

On the 5th of November, 1661 it kept a mighty noise, and a servant observing two boards in the Children's room seeming to move, he bid it give him one of them. Upon which the Board came (nothing moving it that he saw) within a yard of him. The Man added, "Nay, let me have it in my Hand." Upon which it was shov'd quite home to him. He thrust it back, and it was driven to him again, and so up and down, to and fro, at least twenty times together till Mr. Mompesson forbad his servant such Familiarities. This was in the day-time, and seen by a whole Room full of people. That morning it left a sulpherous smell behind it, which was very offensive.

At night the Minister, one Mr. Cragg, and divers of the Neighbours came to the House on a visit. The Minister went to Prayers with them, kneeling at the Childrens Bed-side where it was then very troublesome and loud. During Prayer-time it withdrew into the Cock-loft, but returned as soon as Prayers were done, and then in the sight of the

Company the Chairs walkt about the Room of themselves, the Childrens shooes were hurled over their Heads and every loose thing moved about the Chamber. At the same time a Bedstaff was thrown at the Minister, which hit him on the Leg, but so favourably that a Lock of Wooll could not have fallen more softly, and it was observed that it stopt just where it lighted without rolling or moving from the place.

Mr. Mompesson perceiving that it so much persecuted the little Children, he lodged them out at a Neighbours House, taking his Eldest Daughter, who was about Ten years of age, into his own Chamber, where it had not been a Month before. As soon as she was in Bed the disturbances begun there again, continuing three Weeks Drumming and making other noises, and it was observed that it would exactly answer in Drumming any thing that was beaten or called for. After this, the House where the Children were Lodged out happening to be full of strangers, they were taken home, and no disturbance having been known in the Parlour, they were lodged there, where also their Persecutor found them, but then only pluckt them by the Hair and Nightcloaths, without any other disturbance.

It was noted that when the noise was loudest and came with the most sudden and surprising violence no Dog about the House would move, though the knocking was oft so boisterous and rude that it hath been heard at a considerable distance in the Fields and awakened the Neighbours in the Village, none of which live very near this House. The Servants sometimes were lift up with their Beds, and then let gently down again without hurt. At other times it would lie like a great weight upon their Feet.

About the latter end of December, 1661 the Drummings were less frequent, and then they heard a noise like the gingling of Money, occasioned, as it was thought, by somewhat Mr. Mompesson's Mother had spoken the day before to a Neighbour who talkt of Fayries leaving Money, viz. that she should like it well if it would leave them some to make amends for their trouble. The night after the speaking of which, there was a great clinking of Money over all the House.

After this it desisted from the ruder noises and employed

itself in little Apish and less troublesome Tricks. On Christmas Eve a little before day, one of the little Boys arising out of his Bed was hit on a sore place upon his Heel with the Latch of the Door. The Pin that it was fastened with was so small that it was a difficult matter to pick it out. The night after Christmas day it threw the old Gentlewoman's Cloaths about the Room and hid her Bible in the Ashes. In such silly tricks it was frequent.

After this it was very troublesome to a Servant of Mr. Mompesson's, who was a stout Fellow and of sober Conversation. This Man lay within during the greatest disturbances, and for several nights something would endeavour to pluck his Cloaths off the Bed, so that he was fain to tug hard to keep them on, and sometimes they would be pluckt from him by main force, and his shoes thrown at his head. And now and then he would find himself forcibly held, as it were, bound Hand and Foot, but he found that whenever he could make use of his Sword, and struck with it, the Spirit quitted its hold.

A little after these contests, a Son of Sir Thomas Bennet, whose Workman the Drummer had sometimes been, came to the House, and told Mr. Mompesson some words that he had spoken, which it seems was not well taken. For as soon as they were in Bed the Drum was beat up very violently and loudly. The Gentleman arose and called his Man to him, who lay with Mr. Mompesson's Servant just now spoken of, whose name was John. As soon as Mr. Bennet's man was gone, John heard a rushing noise in his Chamber, and something came to his Bedside as if it had been one in Silk. The Man presently reacheth after his Sword, which he found held from him, and 'twas with difficulty and much tugging that he got it into his power, which as soon as he had done, the Spectre left him, and it was always observed that it still avoided a Sword.

About the beginning of January, 1662 they were wont to hear a Singing in the Chimney before it came down. And one night about this time Lights were seen in the House. One of them came into Mr. Mompesson's Chamber which seemed blue and glimmering, and caused great stiffness in the Eyes of those that saw it. After the Light something was heard coming up the Stairs, as if it had been one without Shooes. The Light was seen also four or five times in the Childrens Chamber, and the Maids confidently affirm that the Doors were at least ten times opened and shut in their sight, and when they were opened they heard a noise as if half a dozen had entered together. After which some were heard to walk about the Room, and one rusled as if it had been in silk. The like Mr. Mompesson himself once heard.

During the time of the knocking, when many were present, a Gentleman of the Company said, "Satan, if the Drummer set thee to work, give three knocks and no more." Which it did very distinctly and stopt. The Gentleman knockt to see if it would answer him as it was wont, but it did not. Fur further trial, he bid it for confirmation, if it were the Drummer, to give five knocks and no more that night, which it did and left the House quiet all the night after. This was done in the presence of Sir Thomas Chamberlain of Oxfordshire, and divers others.

On Saturday Morning, an hour before day, January 10, a Drum was heard beat upon the outsides of Mr. Mompesson's chamber, from whence it went to the other end of the House where some Gentleman strangers lay, playing at their door and without four or five several Tunes, and so went off into the air.

The next night a Smith in the Village lying with John, the Man, they heard a noise in the room as if one had been shoeing of an Horse, and somewhat came as it were with a pair of Pincers, snipping at the Smiths nose most part of the night.

One morning Mr. Mompesson rising early to go a Journey, heard a great noise below where the Children lay, and running down with a Pistol in his hand, he heard a Voice crying, "A Witch, a Witch," as they had also heard it once before. Upon his entrance all was quiet.

Having one Night played some little tricks at Mr. Mompesson's Beds feet, it went into another Bed where one of his Daughters lay. There it passed from side to side, lifting her up as it passed under. At that time there were three kinds of noises in the Bed. They endeavoured to thrust at it with a sword, but it still shifted and carefully avoided the thrust, still getting under the Child when they offered at it. The night after it came panting like a Dog out of breath. Upon which one took a Bedstaff to knock, which was caught out of her hand and thrown away, and company coming up, the room was presently filled with a bloomy noisome smell, and was very hot, though without fire, in a very sharp and severe winter. It continued in the Bed, panting and scratching, an hour and a half, and then went into the next Chamber where it knockt a little and seemed to rattle a Chain. Thus it did for two and three nights together.

After this the old Gentlewomans Bible was found in the Ashes, the Paper side being downwards. Mr. Mompesson took it up, and observed that it lay open at the third Chapter of St. Mark, where there is mention of the unclean Spirit falling down before our Saviour, and of his giving power to the Twelve to cast out Devils, and of the Scribes Opinion that he cast them out through Beelzebub. The next night they strewed Ashes over the Chamber to see what impressions it would leave. In the morning they found in one place the resemblance of a great Claw, in another of a lesser, some Letters in another, which they could make nothing of, besides many Circles and Scratches in the Ashes.

About this time I went to the House on purpose to inquire the truth of these passages, of which there was so loud a report. It had ceased from its Drumming and ruder noises before I came thither, but most of the more remarkable circumstances before related were confirmed to me there by several of the Neighbours together, who had been present at them. At this time it used to haunt the Children, and that as soon as they were laid.

They went to Bed that Night I was there about Eight of the Clock, when a Maid-servant coming down from them told us it was come. The neighbours that were there and two Ministers who had seen and heard divers times went away, but Mr. Mompesson and I and a Gentleman that came with me went up. I heard a strange scratching as I went up the Stairs, and when we came into the Room I perceived it was just behind the Bolster of the Childrens Bed, and seemed to be against the Tick. It was as loud a scratching as one with long Nails could make upon a Bolster.

There were two little modest Girls in the Bed, between Seven and Eleven years old as I guest. I saw their hands out of the Cloaths, and they could not contribute to the noise that was behind their heads. They had been used to it, and had still some body or other in the Chamber with them, and therefore seemed not to be much affrighted.

I standing at the Beds-head, thrust my hand behind the Bolster, directing it to the place whence the noise seemed to come. Whereupon the noise ceased there, and was heard in another part of the Bed. But when I had taken out my hand it returned, and was heard in the same place as before. I had been told that it would imitate noises, and made trial by scratching several times upon the Sheet, as 5 and 7 and 10, which it followed and still stopt at my number. I searched under and behind the Bed, turned up the Cloaths to the Bed-cords, graspt the Bolster, sounded the Wall behind, and made all the search that possibly I could to find if there were any trick, contrivance or common cause of it. The like did my Friend, but we could discover nothing. So that I was then verily perswaded, and am so still, that the noise was made by some Daemon or Spirit. After it had scracht about half an hour or more, it went into the midst of the Bed under the Children, and there seemed to pant like a Dog out of breath very loudly. I put my hand upon the place, and felt the Bed beating up against it as if something within had thrust it up. I graspt the Feathers to feel if any living thing were in it. I looked under and every where about to see if there were any Dog or Cat, or any such Creature in the Room, and so we all did, but found nothing. The motion it caused by this panting was so strong that it shook the Room and Windows very sensibly. It continued thus more than half an hour while my Friend and I staid in the Room, and as long after, as we were told.

During the panting I chanced to see as it had been something (which I thought was a Rat or Mouse) moving in a Linnen Bag that hung up against another Bed that was in the Room. I stept and caught it by the upper end with one Hand, with which I held it and drew it through the other, but found nothing at all in it. There was no body near to shake the Bag, or if there had, no one could have made such motion, which seemed to be from within, as if a Living Creature had moved in it.

This passage I mention not in the former Editions, because it depended upon my single Testimony and might be subject to more evasions than the other I related. But having told it to divers Learned and inquisitive Men who thought it not altogether inconsiderable, I have now added it here.

It will I know be said by some that my Friend and I were under some Affright, and so fancied noises and sights that were not. This is the Eternal Evasion. But if it be possible to know how a Man is affected when in fear and when unconcerned, I certainly know for mine own part that during the whole time of my being in the Room and in the House I was under no more affrightment than I am while I write this Relation. And if I know that I am now awake and that I see the Objects that are before me, I know that I heard and saw the particulars I have told. There is, I am sensible, no great matter for story in them, but there is so much as convinceth me that there was somewhat extraordinary and what we usually call preternatural in the business.

There were other passages at my being in Tedworth which I published not because they are not such plain and unexceptionable Proofs. I shall now briefly mention them, *valeant quantum valere possunt.* My Friend and I lay in the Chamber where the first and chief disturbance had been. We slept well all night, but early before day in the Morning I was awakened (and I believe my Bedfellow) by a great knocking just without our Chamber door. I askt who was there several times, but the knocking still continued without answer. At last I said, "In the Name of God, who is it and what would you have?"

To which a Voice answered, "Nothing with you." We, thinking it had been some Servant of the House, went to sleep again. But speaking of it to Mr. Mompesson when we came down, he assured us that no one of the House lay that way or had business thereabout, and that his Servants were not up till he called them, which was after it was day. Which they confirmed, and protested that the noise was not made by them.

Mr. Mompesson had told us before that it would be gone in the middle of the night and come again divers times early in the Morning, about Four a Clock, and this I suppose was about that time.

Another passage was this. My Man coming up to me in the Morning, told me that one of my Horses (that on which I rode) was all in a sweat and lookt as if he had been rid all night. My Friend and I went down and found him so. I enquired how he had been used, and was assured that he had been well fed and ordered as he used to be, and my Servant was one that was wont to be very careful about my Horses. The Horse I had had a good time, and never knew but that he was very sound. But after I had rid him a Mile or two very gently over a plain Down from Mr. Mompesson's House, he fell lame, and having made a hard shift to bring me home, died in two or three days, no one being able to imagine what he ailed. This I confess might be accident or some unusual distemper, but all things being put together, it seems very probably that it was somewhat else.

But I go on with Mr. Mompesson's own particulars. There came one Morning a light into the Childrens Chamber and a Voice crying, "A Witch, a Witch," for at least a hundred times together.

Mr. Mompesson at another time (being in the day) seeing some Wood move in the Chimney of the Room where he was, as of itself, discharged a Pistol into it, after which they found several drops of Blood on the Hearth and in divers places of the Stairs.

For two or three nights after the discharge of the Pistol there was calm in the House, but then it came again, applying it self to a little Child newly taken from Nurse. Which it so persecuted that it would not let the poor Infant rest for two nights together, nor suffer a Candle in the Room, but carry them away lighted up the Chimney or throw them under the Bed. It so scared this Child by leaping upon it that for some hours it could not be recovered out of the fright. So that they were forced again to remove the Children out of the House. The next night after which, something about Mid-night came up the Stairs and knockt at Mr. Mompesson's door, but he lying still, it went up another pair of Stairs to his Man's Chamber to whom it appeared standing at his Beds foot. The exact shape and proportion he could not discover, but he saith he saw a great Body with two red and glaring Eyes, which for some time were fixed steadily upon him, and at length disappeared.

Another night, strangers being present, it purr'd in the Childrens Bed like a Cat, at which time also the Cloaths and Children were lift up from the Bed, and six Men could not keep them down. Hereupon they removed the Children, intending to have ript up the Bed. But they were no sooner laid in another, but the second Bed was more troubled than the first. It continued thus four hours, and so beat the Childrens Leggs against the Bed-posts that they were forced to arise and sit up all night. After this it would empty Chamber-pots into their Beds and strew them with Ashes, though they were never so carefully watcht. It put a long piked Iron into Mr. Mompesson's Bed, and into his Mothers a naked Knife upright. It would fill Porreagers with Ashes, throw every thing about and keep a noise all day.

About the beginning of April 1663 a Gentleman that lay in the House had all his money turned black in his Pockets, and Mr. Mompesson coming one Morning into his Stable, found the Horse he was wont to Ride on the Ground, having one of his hinder Leggs in his Mouth, and so fastened there that it was difficult for several Men to get it out with a Leaver. After this there were some other remarkable things, but my account goes no further. Only Mr. Mompesson writ me word that afterwards the House was several nights beset with seven or eight in the shape of Men who, as soon as a Gun was discharged would shuffle away together into an Arbour.

The Drummer was tryed at the Assizes at Salisbury upon this occasion. He was committed first to Gloucester Gaol for stealing, and a Wiltshire Man coming to see him, he askt what news in Wiltshire. The Visitant said he knew of none.

"No," saith the Drummer. "Do not you hear of the Drumming at a Gentlemans House at Tedworth?"

"That I do enough," saith the other.

"I," quoth the Drummer, "I have plagued him" (or to that purpose), "and he shall never be quiet till he hath made me satisfaction for taking away my Drum."

Upon Information of this, the Fellow was tryed for a Witch at Sarum, and all the main circumstances I have related were sworn at the Assizes by the Minister of the Parish, and divers others of the most intelligent and substantial Inhabitants who had been Eye and Ear-witnesses of them time after time for divers years together.

The fellow was condemned to Transportation, and accordingly sent away, but I know not how ('tis said by raising storms and affrighting the Seamen) he made shift to come back again. And 'tis observable that during all the time of his restraint and absence the House was quiet, but as soon as ever he came back at liberty the disturbance returned.

He had been a Souldier under Cromwel, and used to talk much of Gallant Books he had of an odd Fellow who was counted a Wizzard. Upon this occasion I shall here add a passage which I had not from Mr. Mompesson, but yet relates to the main purpose.

The Gentleman who was with me at the House, Mr. Hill, being in company with one Compton of Somersetshire who practised Physick and pretends to strange matters, related to him this story of Mr. Mompesson's disturbance. The Physician told him he was sure it was nothing but a Rendezvous of Witches, and that for an hundred pounds he would undertake to rid the House of all disturbance. In pursuit of this discourse, he talkt of many high things, and having drawn my Friend into another Room apart from the rest of the Company, said he would make him sensible he could do something more than ordinary, and askt him who he desired to see.

Mr. Hill had no great confidence in his talk, but yet being earnestly prest to name some one, He said he desired to see no one so much as his Wife who was then many miles distant from them at her home. Upon this, Compton took up a Looking-glass that was in the Room, and setting it down again, bid my friend look in it. Which he did, and there as he most solemnly and seriously professeth, he saw the exact image of his Wife in that habit which she then wore, and working at her Needle in such a part of the Room (there represented also) in which and about which time she really was, as he found upon enquiry when he came home. The

Gentleman himself averred this to me, and he is a very sober, intelligent and credible person. Compton had no knowledge of him before, and was an utter stranger to the person of his Wife. The same man we shall meet again in the story of the Witchcrafts of Elizabeth Style, whom he discovered to be a Witch by foretelling her coming into an House and going out again without speaking . . . He was by all accounted a very odd person.

Thus I have written the summ of Mr. Mompesson's disturbance, which I had partly from his own mouth related before divers who had been witnesses of all and confirmed his relation, and partly from his own Letters, from which the order and series of things is taken. The same particulars he also writ to Dr. Creed, then Doctor of the Chair in Oxford.*

Mr. Mompesson is a Gentleman of whose truth in this account I have not the least ground of suspicion, he being neither vain nor credulous, but a discreet, sagacious and manly person. Now the credit of matters of Fact depends much upon the Relators, who, if they cannot be deceived themselves nor supposed any ways interested to impose upon others, ought to be credited. For upon these circumstances all humane Faith is grounded, and matter of Fact is not capable of any proof besides but that of immediate sensible evidence.

Now this Gentleman cannot be thought ignorant whether that he relates be true or no, the Scene of all being his own House, himself a witness, and that not of a circumstance or two, but of an hundred, nor for once or twice only, but for the space of some years, during which he was a concerned and inquisitive Observer. So that it cannot with any show of reason be supposed that any of his Servants abused him, since in all that time he must needs have detected the deceit.

And what interest could any of his Family have had (if it had been possible to have managed without discovery) to continue so long, so troublesome and so injurious an Imposture? Nor can it with any whit of more probability be imagined that his own melancholy deluded him, since

---

*This would be Dr. William Creed (1614-1663), Regius Professor of Divinity at Oxford and Archdeacon of Wiltshire.

(besides that he is no crazy nor imaginative person) that humour could not have been so lasting and pertinacious. Or if it were so in him, can we think he infected his whole Family and those multitudes of Neighbours and others who had so often been Witnesses of those passages? Such Supposals are wild, and not like to tempt any but those whose Wills are their Reasons. So that upon the whole, the principal Relator, Mr. Mompesson himself, knew whether what He reports was true or not, whether those things acted in his House were contrived Cheats or extraordinary Realities. And if so, what Interest could he serve in carrying on or conniving at a jugling Design and Imposture?

He suffered by it in his Name, in his Estate, in all his Affairs and in the general Peace of his Family. The unbelievers in the matter of Spirits and Witches took him for an Impostor. Many others judged the Permission of such an extraordinary Evil to be the Judgement of God upon him for some notorious wickedness or impiety. Thus his Name was continuously exposed to Censure, and his Estate suffered by the Concourse of People from all parts to his House, by the Diversion it gave him from his Affairs, by the Discouragement of Servants, by reason of which he could hardly get any to live with him. To which if I add the continuall Hurry that his Family was in, the Affrights, Vexations and Tossings up and down of his Children, and the Watchings and Disturbance of his whole House (in all which Himself must needs be the most concerned) I say, if these things are considered, there will be little reason to think he could have any Interest to put a Cheat upon the World in which he would most of all have injured and abused Himself. Or if he should have designed and managed so incredible, so unprofitable a Delusion, 'tis strange that he should have troubled himself so long in such a Business only to deceive and be talkt of. And it is yet more so that none of those many inquisitive Persons that came thither purposely to criticize and examine the Truth of those Matters could make any Discoveries of the Juggling, especially since many came prejudiced against the Belief of such things in general, and others resolved beforehand against the Belief of this, and all were permitted the utmost Freedom of Search and Enquiry.

And after Things were weighed and examined, some that were before greatly prejudiced went away fully convinced. To all which I add that:

There are divers Particulars in the Story in which no Abuse or Deceit could have been practised, as the Motion of Boards and Chairs of themselves, the beating of a Drum in the midst of a Room and in the Air when nothing was to be seen, the great Heat in in a Chamber that had no Fire in excessive cold weather, the Scratching and Panting, the violent Beating and Shaking of the Bedsteads, of which there was no perceivable Cause or Occasion: in these and such like Instances it is not to be conceived how Tricks could have been put upon so Many, so Jealous and so Inquisitive Persons as were Witnesses of them.

'Tis true that when the Gentlemen the King sent were there the House was quiet, and nothing seen nor heard that night, which was confidently and with triumph urged by many as a confutation of the story. But 'twas bad Logick to conclude in matters of Fact from a single Negative, and such a one against numerous Affirmatives, and so affirm that a thing was never done because not at such a particular time, or that no body ever saw what this Man or that did not. By the same way of reasoning I may infer that there were never any Robberies done on Salisbury Plain, Hownslow Heath or the other noted places because I have often Travelled all those ways and yet was never Robbed. And the Spaniard inferred well that said there was no Sun in England because he had been six weeks here and never saw it. This is the common argument of those that deny the Being of Apparitions. They have Travelled all hours of the night, and never saw any thing worse than themselves (which may well be), and thence they conclude that all pretended Apparitions are Fancies or Impostures. But why do not such arguers conclude that there was never a Cut-purse in London because they have lived there many years without being met by any of those Practisers? Certainly he that denies Apparitions upon the confidence of this Negative against the vast heap of Positive Assurances is credulous in believing that there was ever any Highway-man in the World if he himself was never Robb'd. And the Trials of Assizes and Attestations of those who have (if he will be just) ought to move his assent no more in this case than in that of Witches and Apparitions, which have the very same evidence.

But as to the quiet of Mr. Mompesson's House when the Courtiers were there, it may be remembered and considered that the disturbance was not constant, but intermitted sometimes several days, sometimes weeks. So that the intermission at that time might be accidental, or perhaps the Daemon was not willing to give so publick a Testimony of those Transactions which possibly might convince those who he had rather should continue in the unbelief of his existence. But however it were, this circumstance will afford but a very slender inference against the credit of the story, except among those who are willing to take any thing for an Argument against things which they have an interest not to acknowledge.

I have thus related the sum of the story, and noted some circumstances that assure the truth of it. I confess the passages recited are not so dreadful, tragical and amazing as there are some in story of this kind, yet are they never the less probable or true for their being not so prodigious and astonishing.

And they are strange enough to prove themselves effects of some invisible extraordinary Agent, and so demonstrate that there are Spirits who sometimes sensibly intermeddle in our affairs. And I think they do it with clearness of evidence. For these things were not done long ago or at far distance, in an ignorant age or among a barbarous people. They were not seen by two or three only of the Melancholick and superstitious, and reported by those that made them serve the advantage and interest of a party. They were not the passages of a Day or Night, nor the vanishing glances of an Apparition. But these Transactions were near and late, publick, frequent and of divers years continuance, witnessed by multitudes of competent and unbyassed Attestors, and acted in a searching, incredulous Age: Arguments enough, one would think, to convince any modest and capable reason.

—*Saducismus triumphatus*

87. The Examination of Christian Green

Which is the Examination and Confession of Christian Green, aged about thirty three years, Wife of Robert Green of Brewham in the County of Somerset, taken before Robert Hunt, Esq; March 2, 1664.

This Examinant saith that about a year and a half since (she being in great poverty) one Catherine Green of Brewham told her that if she would, she might be in a better condition, and then perswaded her to make a Covenant with the Devil. Being afterwards together in Mr. Hussey's Ground in Brewham Forest about Noon, Catherine called for the Devil who appeared in the shape of a Man in blackish Cloths, and said somewhat to Catherine which Christian could not hear. After which, the Devil (as she conceived him) told the Examinant that she should want neither Cloths, Victual nor Money if she would give her Body and Soul to him, keep his Secrets and suffer him to suck her once in twenty four hours. Which at last, upon his and Catherine Green's perswasion she yielded to. Then the Man in black prickt the fourth Finger of her Right hand, between the middle and upper Joints, where the sign yet remains, and took two drops of her blood on his Finger, giving her four-pence-half-penny with which she after bought Bread in Brewham. Then he spake again in private with Catherine and vanished, leaving a smell of Brimstone behind.

Since that time the Devil (she saith) hath and doth usually suck her left Breast about five of the Clock in the Morning in the likeness of an Hedge-hog bending, and did so on Wednesday Morning last. She saith it is painful to her, and that she is usually in a trance when she is suckt.

She saith also that Catherine Green and Margaret Agar of Brewham have told her that they are in Covenant with the Devil, and confesseth that she hath been at several meetings in the Night at Brewham Common and in a Ground of Mr. Hussey's, that she hath there met with Catherine Green and Margaret Agar, and three or four times with Mary

Warberton of Brewham. That in all those meetings the Devil hath been present in the shape of a Man in black Cloths. At their first coming he bids them welcome, but always speaks very low.

That at a Meeting about three Weeks or a Month since, at or near the former place, Margaret Agar brought thither an Image in Wax for Elizabeth, the Wife of Andrew Cornish of Brewham, and the Devil in the shape of a Man in black Cloths did Baptize it, and after stuck a Thorn into its Head. That Agar stuck one into its Stomach, and Catherine Green one into its side. She further saith that before this time Agar said to her, this Examinant, that she would hurt Eliz. Cornish, who since the Baptizing of the Picture hath been taken and continues very ill.

She saith that three or four days before Jos. Talbot of Brewham died, Margaret Agar told her that she would rid him out of the World because he, being Overseer of the Poor, made her children go to Service and refused to give them such good Cloths as she desired. And since the Death of Talbot, she confessed to the Examinant that she had bewitcht him to death. He died about a year since, was taken ill on Friday and died about Wednesday after.

That her Mother-in-law, Catherine Green, about five or six years ago was taken in a strange manner. One day one Eye and Cheek did swell, another day another, and so she continued in great pain till she died. Upon her death she several times said in the hearing of the Examinant that her Sister-in-law, Catherine Green, had bewitched her, and the Examinant believes that she bewticht her to Death.

That a little before Michaelmas last the said Catherine cursed the Horses of Rob. Walter of Brewham, saying, "A Murrain on them Horses to Death." Upon which the Horses, being three, all died.

       Taken before me,
        Rob. Hunt.

Elizabeth Talbot of Brewham, Examined March 7, 1664, before Robert Hunt, Esq; saith that about three Weeks before her Father, Jos. Talbot, died, Margaret Agar fell out with him because he, being Overseer for the Poor, did require Agars Daughter to go to Service, and said to him that he was proud of his living, but swore by the Blood of the Lord that he should not long enjoy it. Within three Weeks of which he was suddenly taken in his Body as if he had been stabb'd with Daggers, and so continued four or five days in great pain, and then died.

ROB. HUNT.

Jos. Smith of Brewham, Husbandman, Examined March 15, 1664 before Rob. Hunt, Esq; saith that some few days before Jos. Talbot died, he heard Margaret Agar rail very much at him because he had caused her daughter to go to Service, and said that he should not keep his living, but be drawn out upon four Mens shoulders. That she would tread upon his Jaws and see the grass over his head, which she swore by the Blood of the Lord.

Taken upon Oath before
ROB. HUNT.

Mary, the Wife of William Smith of Brewham, Examined March 8, 1664 before Rob. Hunt, Esq; saith that about two years since, Margaret Agar came to her and called her Whore, adding, "A Plague take you for an old Whore. I shall live to see thee rot on the Earth before I die, and thy Cows shall fall and die at my feet. A short time after which, she had three Cows that died very strangely, and two of them at the door of Margaret Agar. And ever since, the Examinant hath consumed and pined away, her Body and her Bowels rotting, and she verily believes that her Cattle and her self were bewitched by Agar.

Taken upon Oath before
ROB. HUNT.

Catherine Green, alias Cornish of Brewham, Examined May 16, 1665 before Rob. Hunt, Esq; saith that on Friday in the Evening in the beginning of March last, Margaret Agar came to her and was earnest she should go with her to a Ground called Husseys-knap, which she did, and being come thither, they saw a little Man in black Cloths, with a little Band. As soon as they came to him, Margaret Agar took out of her Lap a little Picture in blackish Wax which she delivered to the Man in black, who stuck a Thorn into the Crown of the Picture and then delivered it back to Agar. Upon which she stuck a Thorn towards the heart of the Picture, cursing and saying, "A Plague on you," which she told the Examinant was done to hurt Eliz. Cornish, who as she hath been told hath been very ill since that time.

That a little above a year since, Jos. Talbot, late of Brewham, being Overseer for the Poor, did cause two of Agar's Children to go to Service. Upon which she was very angry, and said in the Examinant's hearing a few days before he fell sick and died that she had trod upon the Jaws of three of her Enemies, and that she should shortly see Talbot rot, and tread on his Jaws. And when this Examinant desired her not to hurt Talbot, she swore by the Blood of the Lord she would confound him if she could. The day before he died, she said to this Examinant, "God's wounds, I'll go and see him, for I shall never see him more." And the next day Talbot died.

That she heard Margaret Agar curse Mary Smith, and say she should live to see her and her Cattle fall and rot before her face.

Taken upon Oath before
Rob. Hunt.

Mary Green of Brewham, single Woman, examined June 3, 1665 before Rob. Hunt, Esq; saith that about a Month before Jos. Talbot late of Brewham died, Margaret Agar fell out with him about the putting of her Child to Service. After that she saw a Picture in Clay or Wax in the hands of Agar, which she said was for Talbot. The Picture she saw her deliver in Redmore to the Fiend in the shape of a Man in black about an Hour in the Night, who stuck a Thorn in or near the Heart of it. Agar stuck another in the Breast, and Catherine Green, Alice Green, Mary Warberton, Henry Walter and Christian Green, all of Brewham, were then and there present, and did all stick Thorns into the Picture.

At that time Catherine Green spake to Agar not to hurt Talbot because she received somewhat from him often Times, but Agar replied, by the Lord's Blood she would confound him, or words to that Purpose.

That a little before Talbot was taken sick, Agar being in the House where the Examinant lived, swore that she should ere long tread upon his Jaws, yet if she came home in a quarter it would be time enough to see him carried out upon four Mens shoulders, and to tread upon his Jaws.

That on the day Talbot dyed she heard Agar swear that

she had now plagued Talbot, and that being in Company with her some time before, and seeing a dead Horse of Talbot's drawn along by another of his Horses, she swore that that Horse should be also drawn out tomorrow, and the next day she saw the well Horse also drawn out dead.

That about a Month before Margaret Agar was sent to Gaol, she saw her, Henry Walter, Catherine Green, Joan Syms, Christian Green, Mary Warberton and others meet at a place called Hussey's-knap in the Forest in the Night time, where met them the Fiend in the shape of a little Man in black Cloths with a little Band. To him all made obeysances, and at that time a Picture in Wax or Clay was delivered by Agar to the Man in black, who stuck a Thorn into the Crown of it, Margaret Agar one towards the Breast, Catherine Green in the side, after which Agar threw down the Picture and said, "There is Cornish's Picture with a Murrain to it," or Plague on it. And that at both the meetings there was a noisome smell of Brimstone.

That about two years since in the Night there met in the same place Agar, Henry Walter, Catherine Green, Joan Syms, Alice Green and Mary Warberton. Then also Margaret Agar delivered to the little Man in black a Picture in Wax, into which he and Agar stuck Thorns, and Henry Walter thrust his Thumb into the side of it. Then they threw it down and said, "There is Dick Green's Picture with a Pox in't." A short time after which Richard Green was taken ill and died.

Further she saith that on Thursday Night before Whitsunday last about the same place met Catherine Green, Alice Green, Joan Syms, Mary Warberton, Dinah and Dorothy Warberton and Henry Walter, and being met they called out Robin. Upon which instantly appeared a little Man in black Cloths, to whom all made obeysance. And the little Man put his hand to his Hat, saying, "How do ye?" speaking low but big. Then all made low obeysances to him again. That she hath seen Margaret Clark twice at the meetings, but since Margaret Agar was sent to Prison she never saw her there.

Taken before me
ROB. HUNT.
—*Saducismus triumphatus*

*   *   *

Witchcraft, causing illness or death by the use of an image, has of course been common all over the world. In all magic, in all primitive sacrifice, like has been thought to attract like. I once knew an old Russian lady who had hated her piano teacher when she was a child. She had made a wax figure of him and stuck pins into it. A few days later he died of appendicitis, and she went to his funeral holding her father's hand. Seventy years afterward one of her vividest memories was of that day when she had expected at any moment to be arrested for murder.

88. Image Witchcraft Among Australian Aborigines

If the members of one (aboriginal) tribe wished to work harm on one of another tribe, the men would leave their camp, and select a secluded sandy spot; they would then make a depression in the sand in the centre of which a rude figure of a man is moulded. By concentrating their thoughts on the one they desire to harm, and by singing a weird song the mischief is wrought. The subject of their animosity will develop a high fever and will probable die within a day or two.

—W. H. BIRD, in *Anthropos,* vi

89. The Ordeal of the Old Man of Mpete

Kiala, the chief of the town, had relatives in Mpete, a town two hours distant; one of them died, and the accusation of the cause of the death by witchcraft was fastened on an old man of Mpete.

Kiala and his party urged that he should take *nkasa* (a

poison). There had been no intervention of a witch doctor, but the old man had outlived all his generation and the people said that he survived because he was the cause of the death of all of them; he was the witch, so of course he survived. We cautioned Kiala, and he was afraid to let things take their usual course for fear of the State; he therefore determined to put him to death without actually killing him. He took a party up to Mpete one moonlight night, caught the old man in his house and bound him. They dug a hole in front of the house, put the old man in, and buried him alive. If he died it was his business; nobody had killed him.

—W. H. BENTLEY, *Pioneering in the Congo*, ii

90. Eighteen Witches Drowned in the Congo

A canoe from Vivi with six people in it was descending the river . . . As they rounded the point upon which afterwards our Underhill station was built, the canoe was caught in a cauldron, filled and sank. . . The natives . . . decided that the witchcraft which caused so terrible an accident was no ordinary witchcraft, and must be met accordingly. Three witches must die for each man drowned, so that eighteen more must be put to death because of an accident which had caused the drowning of six men! In that district, deaths of important men or under extraordinary circumstances, were so met.

—*Pioneering in the Congo*

91. The Deposition of Elizabeth Style

Elizabeth Style of Stoke Trister in the County of Somerset was accused by divers Persons of Credit upon Oath before Mr. Hunt, and particularly and largely confessed her guilt herself, which was found by the Jury at her Trial at Taunton. But she prevented

Execution by dying in Gaol a little before the expiring of the term her Confederate Daemon had set for her enjoyment of Diabolical pleasures in this life. I have shortned the Examinations, and cast them into such an order as I think fittest for the rendring the matter clear and intelligible.

Rich. Hill of Stoke Trister in the County of Somerset, Yeoman, being Examined upon Oath Jan. 23, 1664 before Rob. Hunt, Esq; one of his Majesty's Justices for that County, concerning the bewitching of his daughter by Eliz. Style, declareth that his Daughter, Eliz. Hill, about the age of 13 years, hath been for about two Months last past taken with very strange Fits, which have held an hour, two, three and more; and that in those Fits the Child hath told her Father, the Examinant, and other, that one Eliz. Style of the same Parish appeared to her, and is the Person that Torments her. She also in her Fits usually tells what Cloths Eliz. Style hath on at that time, which the Informant and others have seen and found true.

He saith further that about a Fortnight before Christmas last he told Style that his Daughter spoke much of her in her Fits, and did Believe that she was bewitched by her. Whereupon Francis White and Walter and Robert Thick being present, willed her to complain to the Justice against him for accusing of her. But she having used several put-offs, said she would do worse than fetch a Warrant. After which the Girl grew worse than before, and at the end of a Fit she tells the Examinant when she shall have another, which happens accordingly, and (she) affirms that Style tells her when the next Fit shall come. He informs further that Munday Night after Christmas-Day about Nine of the Clock, and four or five times since about the same hour of the Night, his Daughter hath been more Tormented than formerly, and that though held in a Chair by four or five People, sometimes six, by the Arms, Legs and Shoulders, she would rise out of her Chair and raise her body about three or four feet high. And after that, in her Fits she would have holes made in her Hand-Wrists, Face, Neck and other parts of her body, which the Informant and others that saw them conceived to be with Thorns. For they saw Thorns in her Flesh, and some they hooked out.

That upon the Childs pointing with her Finger from place to place, the Thorns and Holes immediately appeared to the Informant and others looking on. And as soon as the Child can speak after the Fit, she saith that Widow Style did prick her with Thorns in those several places, which was horrible Torment, and she seemed to the Informant and others standing by to be in extream pain and torture.

The Child hath been so tormented and pricked with Thorns four several Nights, at which times the Informant and many other People have seen the Flesh rise up in little bunches in which Holes did appear. The Pricking held about a quarter of an hour at a time during each of the four Fits, and the Informant hath seen the Child take out some of those Thorns.

The same Rich. Hill, Examined Jan. 26, 1664, informs that when he rode from the Justices House with a Warrant to bring Style before him, his Horse on a suddain sat down on his Breech, and he could not after ride him, but as soon as he attempted to get up, his Horse would sit down and paw with his Feet before. He saith further that since Style was Examined before the Justice and made her Confession to him, she hath acknowledged to the Informant that she had hurt his Daughter, and that one Anne Bishop and Alice Duke did join in bewitching of her.

Taken upon Oath before me,

ROB. HUNT.

William Parsons, Rector of Stoke Trister in the County of Somerset, Examined the 26 of Jan. 1664 before Rob. Hunt, Esq; concerning the bewitching of Rich. Hill's Daughter, saith that on Monday Night after Christmas-Day then last past, he came into the Room when Eliz. Hill was in her Fit, many of his Parishioners being present and looking on. He there saw the Child held in a Chair by main force by the People, plunging far beyond the strength of nature, foaming and catching at her own Arms and Legs with her Teeth. This Fit he conceived held about half an hour. After some time she pointed with her Finger to the left side of her Head, next to her left Arm, and then to her left Hand, &c., and where she pointed he perceived a red spot to arise with a small black in the midst of it like a small Thorn. She pointed also to her

Toes one after the other, and exprest great sense of Torment. This latter Fit he guesses continued about a quarter of an hour, during most or all of which time her Stomach seemed to swell, and her Head where she seemed to be prickt did so very much. She sate foaming much of the time, and the next day after her Fit, she shewed the Examinant the places where the Thorns were stuck in, and he saw the Thorns in those places.

Taken on Oath before me,
ROB. HUNT.

Subscribed,
WILLIAM PARSONS, *Rector of Stoke Trister*

Nicholas Lambert of Bayford in the County of Somerset, Yeoman, Examined upon Oath before Rob. Hunt, Esq; Jan. 30, 1664 concerning the bewitching of Rich. Hill's Daughter by Elizabeth Style, testifieth that Monday after Christmas-Day last, being with others in the House of Rich. Hill, he saw his Daughter Elizabeth taken very ill, and in Fits that were so strong that six Men could not hold her down in a Chair in which she was sat, but that she would raise the Chair up in spite of their utmost force. That in her Fits being not able to speak, she would wrest her body as one in great Torment, and point with her Finger to her Neck, Head, Hand-Wrists, Arms and Toes. And he, with the rest looking on the places to which she pointed, saw on the suddain little Red Spots arise with little black ones in the midst as if Thorns were stuck in them, but the Child then only pointed, without touching her Flesh with her Finger.

Taken upon Oath before me,
ROB. HUNT.

Richard Vining of Stoke Trister, Butcher, Examined Jan. 26, 1664 before Rob. Hunt, Esq; concerning the bewitching of his Wife by Eliz. Style saith that about two or three days before S. James's Day three years since or thereabout, his late wife Agnes fell out with Eliz. Style, and within two or three days after, she was taken with a grievous Pricking in her Thigh, which pain continued for a long time, till after some Physick taken from one Hallet, she was at some Ease for three or four weeks. About the Christmas after the mentioned S. James's day, Style came to the Examinant's house and gave Agnes, his Wife, two Apples, one of them a very fair red Apple, which Style desired her to eat. Which she did, and in a few hours was taken ill and worse than ever she had been before.

Upon this the Examinant went to one M. Compton who lived in the Parish of Ditch Eate (the same Person that shewed my Friend his Wife in a Glass as I have related in the Story of Mr. Mompesson) for Physick for his Wife. Compton told him he could do her no good, for that she was hurt by a near Neighbour who would come into his house and up into the Chamber where his Wife was, but would go out again without speaking.

After Vining came home, being in the Chamber with his Wife, Style came up to them, but went out again without saying a word. Agnes, the Wife, continued in great Pain till Easter Eve following, and then she dyed. Before her Death her Hip rotted, and one of her Eyes swelled out. She declared to him then and at several times before that she believed Eliz. Style had bewitched her, and that she was the Cause of her death.

Taken upon Oath before me,
ROB. HUNT.

Whilst the Justice was examining Style at Wincaunton (which is not above a Mile and a half from Stoke Trister) upon the former Evidence against her, he observed that Rich. Vining looked very earnestly upon him. Whereupon he asked Vining if he had any thing to say unto him.

He answered that Style had bewitched his Wife, and told the Manner how as in his Deposition related. The Woman Style upon this seemed appaled and concerned, and the Justice saying to her, "You have been an old Sinner. You deserve little Mercy," she replied, "I have askt God Mercy for it."

Mr. Hunt askt her why then she would continue in such ill Courses. She said the Devil tempted her, and then began to make some Confession of his Actings with her. Upon this the Justice sent her to the Constable's House at Bayford, which is in the Parish of Stoke Trister (the Constable was one Mr. Gapper), and the next Morning went thither himself, accompanied with two Persons of Quality, Mr. Bull and Mr. Court, now Justices of the Peace in this County.

Now before I proceed further in the Story I shall take notice that here are Three credible Witnesses swearing to the same Particulars, in that the Child Elizabeth Hill was some times in strange Fits in which her strength was encreased beyond the Proportion of Nature and the Force of divers men, that then she pointed to the Parts of her Body where they saw red Spots arising, and black Specks in the midst of them, that she complained she was prickt with Thorns, and two of them saw Thorns in the places of which she complained. Some of which Thorns, one swears that He and Others saw hooked out, and that the Girl her self pulled out others. That in her Fits she declared Style appears to her (as Jane Brooks did to Richard Jones in the former Relation) and tells her when she shall have another Fit, which happens accordingly. That she describes the Cloths the Woman had on exactly as they find.

But notwithstanding, all this shall be Melancholy and Fancy or Legerdemain or natural Distemper, or any thing but Witchcraft. Or the Fact shall be denied and the three Witnesses perjured, though this Confidence against the Oaths of sober Men tend to the Overthrow of all Testimony and History, and the rendring of all Laws useless. I shall therefore proceed to further Proof, and such as will abundantly strengthen this. It is the Confession of Style her self.

I left Mr. Hunt and the other two Gentlemen at the Constable's house where Style was, upon Business of further Examination, where she enlarged upon the Confession she had before begun to make, and declared the whole matter at that and two other times after in the Particulars that follow.

Elizabeth Styles, her Confession of her Witchcrafts, Jan. 26 and 30 and Feb. 7, 1664, before Rob. Hunt, Esq.

She then confessed that the Devil about Ten years since appeared to her in the shape of a handsome Man, and after of a black Dog. That he promised her Money and that she should live gallantly and have the Pleasure of the World for twelve years if she would with her Blood sign his Paper, which was to give her Soul to him and observe his Laws, and that he might suck her Blood.

This after Four Sollicitations the Examinant promised to

do. Upon which he prickt the fourth Finger of her right hand between the middle and upper Joynt (where the Sign at the Examination remained) and with a Drop or two of her Blood she signed the Paper with an O. Upon this the Devil gave her Sixpence and vanished with the Paper.

That since he hath appeared to her in the Shape of a Man, and did so on Wednesday seven-night past, but more usually he appears in the Likeness of a Dog and Cat and a Fly like a Millar, in which last he usually sucks in the Poll about four of the Clock in the Morning, and did so Jan. 27, and that it usually is Pain to her to be so suckt.

That when she hath a desire to do harm she calls the Spirit by the name of Robin, to whom when he appeareth she uses these words: "O Sathan, give me my purpose." She then tells him what she would have done. And that he should so appear to her was part of her Contract with him.

That about a Month ago he appearing, she desired him to torment one Elizabeth Hill and to thrust Thorns into her Flesh, which he promised to do, and the next time he appeared he told her he had done it.

That a little above a Month since this Examinant, Alice Duke, Anne Bishop and Mary Penny met about Nine of the Clock in the Night in the Common near Trister Gate where they met a Man in black Cloths with a little Band, to whom they did Courtesie and due observance, and the Examinant verily believes that this was the Devil.

At that time Alice Duke brought a Picture in Wax, which was for Elizabeth Hill. The Man in black took it in his Arms, anointed its Fore-head and said, "I baptize thee with this Oyl," and used some other words. He was Godfather, and the Examinant and Anne Bishop Godmothers. They called it Elizabeth or Bess. Then the Man in black, this Examinant, Anne Bishop and Alice Duke stuck Thorns into several places of the Neck, Hand-Wrists, Fingers and several other parts of the said Picture. After which they had Wine, Cakes and Rost Meat (all brought by the Man in black) which they did eat and drink. They danced and were merry, were bodily there and in their Cloths.

She further saith that the same persons met again at or near the same place about a Month since, when Anne Bishop brought a Picture in Wax which was Baptized John in like manner as the other was, the Man in black was Godfather and Alice Duke and this Examinant Godmothers. As soon as it was Baptized Anne Bishop stuck two Thorns into the Arms of the Picture, which was for one Robert Newton's Child of Wincaunton. After they had drunk and made merry, they departed.

That she with Anne Bishop and Alice Duke met at another time in the Night in a ground near Marnhul, where also met several other persons. The Devil, then also there in the former shape, Baptized a Picture by the name of Anne or Rachel Hatcher. The Picture one Durnford's Wife brought and stuck Thorns in it. Then they also made merry with Wine and Cakes and so departed.

She saith before they are carried to their meetings they anoint their Foreheads and Hand-Wrists with an Oyl the Spirit brings them (which smells raw) and then they are carried in a very short time, using these words as they pass: *Thout, tout a tout, throughout and about.* And when they go off from their Meetings they say *Rentum tormentum.*

That at their first meeting the Man in black bids them welcome, and they all make low obeysance to him, and he delivers some Wax Candles like little Torches, which they give back again at parting. When they anoint themselves they use a long form of words, and when they stick in Thorns into the Picture of any they would torment, they say *A Pox on thee, I'le spite thee.*

That at every meeting before the Spirit vanisheth away, he appoints the next meeting place and time, and that at his departure there is a foul smell. At their meeting they have usually Wine or good Beer, Cakes, Meat or the like. They eat and drink really when they meet in their Bodies, dance also and have Musick. The Man in black sits at the higher end, and Anne Bishop usually next to him. He useth some words before meat, and none after. His Voice is audible, but very low.

That they are carried some times in their Bodies and their Cloths, sometimes without, and as the Examinant thinks, their Bodies are sometimes left behind. When only their Spirits are present, yet they know one another.

When they would bewitch Man, Woman or Child, they do it sometimes by a Picture made in Wax which the Devil formally Baptizeth. Sometimes they have an Apple, Dish, Spoon, or other thing from their evil Spirit which they give the party to whom they would do harm. Upon which they have power to hurt the person that eats or receives it. Sometimes they have power to do mischief by a touch or curse; by these they can mischief Cattle, and by cursing without touching, but neither without the Devil's leave.

That she hath been at several general meetings in the night at High Common and a Common near Motcombe, at a place called Marnhull, and at other places where they met John Combes, John Vining, Richard Dickes, Thomas Boster or Bolster, Thomas Dunning, James Bush, a lame Man, Rachel King, Richard Lannen, a woman called Durnford, Alice Duke, Anne Bishop, Mary Penny and Christopher Ellen, all which did obeysance to the Man in black, who was at every one of their meetings. Usually they have at them some Picture Baptized.

The Man in black sometimes plays on a Pipe or Cittern, and the Company dance. At last the Devil vanisheth, and all are carried to their several homes in a short space. At their parting they say "A Boy! A merry meet, merry part!"

That the reason why she caused Elizabeth Hill to be the more tormented was because her Father had said she was a Witch. That she has seen Alice Duke's Familiar suck her in the shape of a Cat, and Anne Bishop's suck her in the shape of a Rat.

That she never heard the name of God or Jesus Christ mentioned at any of their meetings.

That Anne Bishop about five years and a half since did bring a Picture in Wax for Robert Newman's Child at Wincaunton.

That some two years ago she gave two Apples to Agnes Vining, late Wife of Richard Vining, and that she had one of the Apples from the Devil, who then appeared to her and told (her) that Apple would do Vining's Wife's business.

Taken in the presence of several grave and Orthodox Divines before me,

ROBERT HUNT.

William Parsons, Rector of Stoke Trister, Examined Feb. 7, 1664 before Rob. Hunt, Esq; concerning Elizabeth Style's Confession saith that he heard Style before the Justice of Peace at the time of her Examination confess, as she hath done also to the Examinant several times since, that she was in Covenant with the Devil, that she had signed it with her Blood, that she had been with the Devil at several meetings in the night, that at one time of those meetings there was brought a Picture in blackish Wax, which the Devil in the shape of a Man in blackish Cloths did Baptize by the name of Eliz. Hill, that she did stick in one Thorn into the Hand-Wrists of the Picture, that Alice Duke stuck Thorns into the same, and that Anne Bishop and Mary Penny were present at that meeting with the Devil.

Taken upon Oath before me,
ROBERT HUNT.
Subscribed,
WILLIAM PARSONS, *Rector of Stoke Trister.*

This Confession of Styles was free and unforced without any torturing or watching, drawn from her by a gentle Examination, meeting with the Convictions of a guilty Conscience. She confesseth that she desired the Devil to torment Eliz. Hill by thrusting Thorns into her Flesh, which he promised, and said he had done it. That a Picture was Baptized for her, the said Elizabeth, and that she, the Familiar and Alice Duke, stuck Thorns into several places of the Neck, Hand-Wrists, Fingers and other parts thereof, which exactly agrees with the strange effects related concerning the torments the Child suffered. And this mischief she confesseth she did because her Father said she was a Witch. She confesseth she gave two Apples to Vining's Wife, one of which she had from the Devil, who said it would do the business, which sutes also with the Testimony of Vining concerning his Wife.

She confesseth further that the Devil useth to suck her in the Poll about four a clock in the Morning in the Form of a Fly like a Millar, concerning which let us hear Testimony. The other particulars of her Confession we shall consider as occasion offers.

Nicholas Lambert, examined again Jan. 26, 1664, before

Rob Hunt, Esq; concerning what happened after Style's Confession, testifyeth that Eliz. Style, having been Examined before the Justices, made her confession and committed to the Officer, the Justice required this Examinant, William Thick and William Read of Bayford to watch her, which they did, and this Informant, sitting near Style by the Fire and reading in the *Practice of Piety,* about Three of the Clock in the Morning there came from her Head a glistering bright Fly about an Inch in length, which pitched at first in the Chimney and then vanished.

In less than a quarter of an hour after there appeared two Flies more of a less size and another colour, which seemed to strike at the Examinant's hand in which he held his Book, but missed it, the one going over, the other under at the same time. He looked stedfastly then on Style, perceived her Countenance to change and to become very black and gastly, the Fire also at the same time changing its colour. Whereupon the Examinant, Thick and Read, conceiving that her Familiar was then about her, looked to her Poll, and seeing her Hair shake very strangely, took it up, and then a Fly like a great Millar flew out from the place and pitched on the Table-board and then vanished away. Upon this, the Examinant and other two persons looking again in Style's Poll, found it very red and like raw Beef. The Examinant askt her what it was that went out of her Poll. She said it was a Butterfly, and askt them why they had not caught it. Lambert said they could not.

"I think so too," answered she.

A little while after, the Informant and the others looking again into her Poll, found the place to be of its former colour. The Examinant demanding again what the Fly was, she confessed it was her Familiar, and that she felt it tickle in her Poll, and that was the usual time when her Familiar came to her.

Taken upon Oath before me,
ROB. HUNT.

Eliz. Torwood of Bayford, Examined Feb. 7, 1664, before Robert Hunt, Esq; concerning the mark found about Eliz. Style after her Confession, deposeth that she, together with Catherine White, Mary Day, Mary Bolster and Bridget Prankard, did a little after Christmas last search Eliz. Style, and that in her Poll they found a little rising which felt hard like a Kernel of Beef, whereupon they suspecting it to be an ill mark, thrust a Pin into it, and having drawn it out, thrust it in again the second time, leaving it sticking in the flesh for some time that the other Women might also see it. Notwithstanding which, Style did neither at the first or second time make the least shew that she felt any thing. But after, when the Constable told her he would thrust a Pin into the place, and made a shew as if he did, "O Lord," said she, "do you prick me," whenas no one then touched her.

The Examinant further saith that Style hath since confessed to her that her Familiar did use to suck her in the place mentioned in the shape of a great Millar, or Butterfly.

Catherine White, Mary Day, Mary Bolster and Bridget Prankard so say that the abovesaid Examination of Eliz. Torwood is truth.

Taken upon Oath before me,
Rob. Hunt.
—Saducismus triumphatus

92. Florence Newton Unable to Pray

Nicholas Stout was next produced by Mr. Attorney-General, who being sworn and Examined, saith that he had often tried her (Florence Newton), having heard say that Witches could not say the Lord's Prayer, whether she could say that Prayer or no, and found she could not. Whereupon she said she could say it, and had oft said it.

And the Court being desired by her to hear her say it, gave her leave. And four times together after these words: *give us this day our daily bread*, she continually said *as we forgive them*, leaving out the words *and forgive us our trespasses*, upon which the Court appointed one near her to teach her these words she so left out. But she either could not, or would not say them, using only these or the like words when these were repeated: *ay, ay, trespasses, that's the words*.

And being often pressed to utter the words as they were

repeated to her, she did not. And being asked the reason, she said she was old and had a bad memory, and being asked how her memory served her so well for other parts of the Prayer, and could not fail her for that, she said she knew not, neither could she help it.
—*Saducismus triumphatus*

93. A Cast of the Bones in South Africa

These practices kill *in ovo* any serious attempt to use reason or experience in the practical life. Native tribes might have arrived at a useful and beneficial knowledge of the medical virtues of plants if they had studied them properly. But what is the use of troubling themselves to study, when a single cast of the bones tells them what root must be taken to cure the disease?
—H. A. JUNOD, *The Life of a South African Tribe*

94. Casting the Bones in the Transvaal

One day I came across some men in a (Transvaal) village who were engaged in throwing the bones (for augury) on a mat spread out on the ground before them. I remarked to them that they were simply gambling and that it would be better if they did not. But one of them replied, "What you call gambling is to us like turning the pages of a book. It is the only one we have. You look at your book every day because you believe what it says. We are doing the same thing. We believe *our* book."
—E. THOMAS, *Le Bokaha,* Bulletin de la Société de Geographie de Neuchâtel, 1895

95. The American Indian Shaman

It is interesting to note that shamans are supposed to have the power of telling at once whether a person has been wrong in any way. They are able to do this because when they look at a person who has stolen or done anything wrong, the person seems to the shaman to be, as it is phrased, 'covered with darkness.'

—R. B. Dixon, *The Shasta*, Bulletin of the American Museum of Natural History

96. East and West African *Muavi*

The Kond is invariably willing to be put to the ordeal, and to drink the *muavi* (poison) is so usual a test that one frequently hears them say, "I will drink *muavi*." They drink *muavi* not only when they want to establish guilt or innocence, but when rights between individuals are in dispute. What is the point in troublesome enquiries when they can so easily find out the truth by letting a cup of *muavi* decide?

—Fullerhorn, *Das deutsche Njassa und Ruwumagebiet in Deutsch Ost Afrika*, x

It is the law that such trials should take place before execution (of the witch). But there is also involved in it another curious fact, and that is that the spirit of the ordeal is held to be able to manage and suppress the bad spirits trained by the witch to destruction. Human beings can collar the witch and destroy him in an examplary manner, but spiritual aid is required to collar the witch's devil, or it would get adrift and carry on after its owner's death.

—Mary Kingsley, *West African Studies*

The decoction itself is supposed to have almost sentience, an ability to feel, in the various organs of the body like a policeman, and detect and destroy the witch spirit supposed to be lurking about.
—R. H. NASSAU, *Fetichism in West Africa*

The priest acts as though he had a supernatural power over the poison. He orders it not to rest in the stomach of the accused if he should be innocent. It must eject itself without doing harm. But if the man is guilty it must cause him to die as he deserves.
—CAVAZZI, *Istoria descrizione de' tre regni Congo, Matamba ed Angola*

* * *

The persecutions in Sweden during the late seventeenth century are famous among historians of witchcraft because here more clearly than elsewhere a link can be established between witchcraft and the vecchia religione *that had lived on in primitive communities since the Iron Age civilizations before the birth of Christ. It is no coincidence that the happenings about to be set down occurred in a district known as Elfdale. Here peasant women, perhaps descendants of the "elves," the primitive remnants, the magic-inducing heirs of Grimm's heroes and heroines in his* Fairy Tales, *describe luxuries they could only have seen in their imaginations. Here, in any case, we shall meet no cursings and demonic possessions, not even pre-Christian or anti-Christian diabolism, but the white and black angels, the dragons, and the magic left over from a time before there were books.*

First a small story of Glanvill's of a witchlike Swedish matricide, to serve as introduction. Then the story of Elfdale itself. If all the threads in this one could be unraveled we should be in a fair way to understanding Merlin and the pre-Christian religion that seems to have been remarkably similar all over northern and western Europe.

97. False Accusation and Death in Stockholm

In the year 1676 at Stockholme a young Woman accused her own Mother of being a Witch, and swore positively that she carried her away at night; whereupon both the Judges and Ministers of the Town exhorted her to Confession and Repentance. But she stifly denied the Allegations, pleaded Innocence, and though they burnt another Witch before her Face and lighted the Fire she herself was to burn in before her, yet she still justified her self, and continued to do so to the last, and continuing so, was burnt.

She had indeed been a very bad Woman, but it seems this crime she was free from, for within a fortnight or three weeks after, her Daughter which had accused her came to the Judges in open Court, weeping and howling, and confessed that she had wronged her Mother, and unjustly out of spleen she had against her for not gratifying her in a thing she desired, had charged her with that Crime which she was innocent of as the Child unborn. Whereupon the Judges gave order for her execution too.

—*Saducismus triumphatus*

98. The Witches of Blockula

A Relation of the Strange Witchcraft Discovered in the Village Mohra in Swedeland in the Years of our Lord 1669 and 1670.

* * *

This account by Anthony Horneck (1641-1697), a German by birth, is printed as an appendix to the 1688 edition of Glanvill's Saducismus triumphatus. *Horneck emigrated to England, became Chaplain of Queen's College, Oxford, Vicar of All Saints' there, and later Chaplain to William III.*

The News of this Witchcraft coming to the King's Ear, his Majesty (Charles XI) was pleased to appoint Commissioners, some of the Clergy and some of the Laity, to make a Journey to the Town aforesaid, and to examine the whole business. And accordingly the Examination was ordered to be on the 13th of August, and the Commissioners met on the 12th instant in the said Village at the Parson's house, to whom both the Minister and several persons of fashion complained with tears in their Eyes of the miserable condition they were in, and therefore begg'd of them to think of some way whereby they might be delivered from that Calamity.

They gave the Commissioners very strange Instances of the Devil's Tyranny among them, how by the help of Witches he had drawn some Hundreds of Children to him and made them subject to his power, how he hath been seen to go in a visible shape through the Country, and appeared daily to the people, how he had wrought upon the poorer sort by presenting them with Meat and Drink, and this way assured them to himself, with other circumstances to be mentioned hereafter.

The Inhabitants of the Village added, with very great Lamentation, that though their Children had told all, and themselves sought God very earnestly by Prayer, yet they were carried away by him, and therefore begg'd of the Lords Commissioners to root out this hellish Crew, that they might regain their former rest and quietness, and the rather because the Children which used to be carried away in the County or District of Elfdale, since some Witches had been burnt there, remained unmolested.

That day, i.e. the 13th of August, being the last Humiliation-day Instituted by Authority for removing of this Judgement, the Commissioners went to Church, where there appeared a considerable Assembly both of young and old. The Children could read, most of them, and sing Psalms, and so could the Women, though not with any great zeal or fervor. There were preached two Sermons that day, in which the miserable case of those people that suffered themselves to be deluded by the Devil was laid open; and these Sermons were at last concluded with very fervent Prayer.

The Publick Worship being over, all the people of the

Town were called together to the Parson's House, near Three thousand of them. Silence being commanded, the King's Commission was read publicky in the hearing of them all, and they were charged under very great Penalties to conceal nothing of what they knew, and to say nothing but the truth, those especially who were guilty, that the Children might be delivered from the Clutches of the Devil. They all promised obedience, the guilty feignedly, but the guiltless weeping and crying bitterly.

On the 14th of August the Commissioners met again, consulting how they might withstand this dangerous Flood. After long deliberation, an Order also coming from his Majesty, they did resolve to execute such as the matter of fact could be proved upon. Examination being made, there were discovered no less than Three-score and ten in the Village aforesaid, Three and twenty of which freely confessing their Crimes, were condemned to Dye. The rest, one pretending she was with Child, and the others denying and pleading not guilty, were sent to Fabluna, where most of them were afterwards Executed.

Fifteen Children which likewise confessed that they were engaged in this Witchery died as the rest. Six and thirty of them between nine and sixteen years of age, who had been less guilty, were forced to run the Gantlet. Twenty more, who had no great inclination, yet had been seduced to those hellish Enterprizes, because they were very young, were Condemned to be lash'd with Rods upon their hands for three Sundays together at the Church-door. And the aforesaid Six and thirty were also doom'd to be lashed this way once a Week for a whole Year together. The number of the Seduced Children was about Three hundred.

On the twenty fifth of August Execution was done upon the notoriously guilty, the day being bright and glorious and the Sun shining, and some thousands of people being present at the Spectacle. The Order and Method observed in the Examination was thus:

First the Commissioners and the Neighbouring Justices went to Prayer. This done, the Witches, who had most of them Children with them which they either had seduced or attempted to seduce, from four years of age to sixteen, were set before them. Some of the Children complained lamentably of the misery and mischief they were forced sometimes to suffer of the Witches.

The Children being asked whether they were sure that they were at any time carried away by the Devil, they all declared they were, begging of the Commissioners that they might be freed from that intolerable Slavery.

Hereupon the Witches themselves were asked whether the Confessions of these Children were true, and admonished to confess the Truth, that they might turn away from the Devil unto the living God. At first most of them did very stiffly, and without shedding the least Tear, deny it, though much against their Will and Inclination.

After this the Children were examined, every one by themselves, to see whether the Confession did agree or no, and the Commissioners found that all of them, except some very little ones who could not tell all the Circumstances, did punctually agree in the confession of Particulars.

In the mean while the Commissioners that were of the Clergy examined the Witches, but could not bring them to any Confession, all continuing stedfast in their denyals, till at last some of them burst out into Tears, and their Confession agreed with what the Children had said. And these ex- press their Abhorrency of the Fact and begg'd pardon, adding that the Devil, whom they call'd *Lacyra,* had stopt the Mouths of some of them, and stopt the Ears of others, and being now gone from them, they could no longer conceal it, for they now perceived his Treachery.

The Confession which the Witches made in Elfdale to the Judges there agreed with the Confession they made at Mohra; and the chief things they confessed consisted in these three Points.

1. Whither they used to go.
2. What kind of place it was they went to, called by them Blockula, where the Witches and the Devil used to meet.
3. What Evil or Mischief they had either done or designed there.

Of their Journey to Blockula. The Contents of their Confession.
We of the Prince of Elfdale do confess that we used to go

to a Gravel-pit which lay hard by a cross-way, and there we put on a Vest over our Heads, and then danced round, and after this ran to the Cross-way and called the Devil thrice, first with a shrill Voice, the second time somewhat louder, and the third time very loud, with these Words: *Antecessour, come and carry us to Blockula.* Whereupon immediately he used to appear, but in different Habits. But for the most part we saw him in a gray Coat and red and blue Stockings. He had a red Beard, a high-crown'd Hat, with Linnen of divers Colours wrapt about it, and long Garters upon his Stockings.

Then he asked us whether we would serve him with Soul and Body. If we were content to do so he set us on a Beast which he had there ready, and carried us over Churches and high Walls, and after all we came to a green Meadow where Blockula lies. We must procure some Scrapings of Altars and Filings of Church Clocks, and then he gives us a Horn with a Salve in it, wherewith we do anoint ourselves, and a Saddle with a Hammer and a wooden Nail. Thereby we fix the Saddle. Whereupon we call upon the Devil, and away we go.

Those that were of the Town of Mohra made in a manner the same Declaration. Being asked whether they were sure of a real personal Transportation and whether they were awake when it was done, they all answered in the Affirmative, and that the Devil sometimes laid something down in the Place that was very like them. But one of them confessed that he did only take away her Strength, and her Body lay still upon the Ground. Yet sometimes he took even her Body with him.

Being asked how they could go with their Bodies through chimneys and broken Panes of Glass, they said that the Devil did first remove all that might hinder them in their flight, and so they had room enough to go.

Others were asked how they were able to carry so many Children with them, and they answered that when the Children were asleep they came into the Chamber, laid hold of the Children which straightway did awake, and asked them whether they would go to a Feast with them. To which some answered yes, others no, yet they were all forced to go. They only gave the Children a Shirt, a Coat and a Doublet which was either red or blue, and so they did set them upon a Beast of the Devil's providing, and then they rid away.

The Children confessed the same thing, and some added that because they had very fine Cloaths put upon them they were very willing to go.

Some of the Children concealed it from their Parents, but others discover'd it to them presently.

The Witches declared moreover that till of late they never had that power to carry away Children, but only this Year and the last, and the Devil did at this time force them to it; that heretofore it was sufficient to carry but one of their Children, or a Stranger's Child with them, which yet happened seldom, but now he did plague them and whip them if they did not procure him Children, insomuch that they had no peace nor quiet for him. And whereas formerly one Journey a Week would serve turn, from their own Town to the place aforesaid, now they were forced to run to other Towns and Places for Children, and that they brought with them, some fifteen, some sixteen Children every night.

For their Journey they said they made of all sorts of Instruments, of Beasts, of Men, of Spits and Posts according as they had opportunity. If they do ride upon Goats and have many Children with them, that all may have Room they stick a Spit into the back-side of the Goat, and then are anointed with the aforesaid Ointment. What the manner of their Journey is, God alone knows. Thus much was made out, that if the Children did at any time name the Names of those that had carried them away, they were again carried by force either to Blockula, or to the Cross-way, and there miserably beaten, insomuch that some of them died of it. And this some of the Witches confessed, and added that now they were exceedingly troubled and tortured in their minds for it.

The Children thus used lookt mighty bleak, wan and beaten. The Marks of the Lashes the Judges could not perceive in them, except in one Boy who had some Wounds and Holes in his Back that were given him with Thorns. But the Witches said they would quickly vanish.

After this usage the Children are exceeding weak, and if any be carried over-night they cannot recover themselves the next day, and they often fall into Fits, the coming of which they know by an extraordinary Paleness that seizes on the

Children, and if a Fit comes upon them they lean on their Mothers Arms, who sit up with them sometimes all night, and when they observe the Paleness coming shake the Children, but to no purpose.

They observe further that their Childrens Breasts grow cold at such times, and they take sometimes a burning Candle and stick it in their hair, which yet is not burnt by it. They swoun upon this paleness, which Swoun lasteth sometimes half an hour, sometimes an hour, sometimes two hours, and when the Children come to themselves again, they mourn and lament and groan most miserably, and beg exceedingly to be eased. This two old Men declared upon Oath before the Judges, and called all the Inhabitants of the Town to witness, as Persons that had most of them experience of this strange Symptome of their Children.

A little Girl of Elfdale confessed that naming the name of Jesus as she was carried away, she fell suddenly upon the Ground, and got a great hole in her Side, which the Devil presently healed up again, and away he carried her. And to this day, the Girl confessed, she had exceeding great pain in her side.

Another Boy confessed too, that one day he was carried away by his Mistress, and to perform the Journey he took his own Fathers Horse out of the Meadow where it was, and upon his return she let the Horse go in her own ground.

The next Morning the Boys Father sought for his Horse, and not finding it, he gave it over for lost. But the Boy told him the whole story, and so his Father fetcht the Horse back again. And this one of the Witches confessed

Of the place where they used to assemble called Blockula, and what they did there.

They unanimously confessed that Blockula is situated in a delicate large Meadow whereof you can see no end. The place, or House they met at, had before it a Gate painted with divers Colours. Through this Gate they went into a little Meadow distinct from the other where the Beasts went that they used to ride on. But the Men whom they made use of in their Journey stood in the House by the Gate in a slumbering posture, sleeping against the Wall.

In a huge large Room of this House, they said, there stood a very long Table at which the Witches did sit down; and that hard by this Room was another Chamber where there were very lovely and delicate Beds.

The first thing they said they must do at Blockula was that they must deny all, and devote themselves Body and Soul to the Devil, and promise to serve him faithfully, and confirm all this with an Oath. Hereupon they cut their Fingers, and with their Blood writ their Name in his Book. They added that he caused them to be Baptized too by such Priests as he had there, and made them confirm their Baptism with dreadful Oaths and Imprecations.

Hereupon the Devil gave them a Purse wherein there were filings of Clocks with a Stone tied to it which they threw into the Water, and then were forced to speak these words: "As these filings of the Clock do never return to the Clock from which they are taken, so may my Soul never return to Heaven." To which they add Blasphemy and other Oaths and Curses.

The mark of their cut Fingers is not found in all of them. But a Girl who had been slashed over her Fingers declared that because she would not stretch out her Finger, the Devil in anger had so cruelly wounded it.

After this they sate down to Table, and those that the Devil esteemed most were placed nearest to him. But the Children must stand at the door, where he himself gives them Meat and Drink.

The Diet they did use to have there was, they said, Broth with Colworts and Bacon in it, Oatmeal, Bread spread with Butter, Milk and Cheese. And they added that sometimes it tasted very well, and sometimes very ill. After Meals they went to Dancing, and in the mean while Swore and Cursed most dreadfully, and afterward went to fighting one with another.

Those of Elfdale confessed that the Devil used to play upon an Harp before them, and afterwards to go with them that he liked best into a Chamber, where he committed venerous Acts with them, and that the Devil had Sons and Daughters by them, which they did Marry together, and they did couple and brought forth Toads and Serpents.

One day the Devil seemed to be dead, whereupon there

were great lamentations at Blockula, but he soon awaked again. If he hath a mind to be merry with them, he lets them all ride upon Spits before him, takes afterwards the Spits and beats them black and blue, and then laughs at them. And he bids them believe that the day of Judgment will come speedily, and therefore sets them to work to build a great House of Stone, promising that in that House he will preserve them from God's Fury, and cause them to enjoy the greatest Delights and Pleasures. But while they work exceeding hard at it, there falls a great part of the Wall down again, whereby some of the Witches are commonly hurt, which makes him laugh, but presently he cures them again.

They said they had seen sometimes a very great Devil like a Dragon with Fire round about him, and bound with an Iron Chain*, and the Devil that converses with them tells them that if they confess any thing he will let that great Devil loose upon them, whereby all Sweedland shall come into great danger.

They added that the Devil had a Church there, such another as in the Town of Mohra. When the Commissioners were coming, he told the Witches they should not fear them, for he would certainly kill them all. And they confessed that some of them had attempted to murther the Commissioners, but had not been able to effect it.

Some of the Children talked much of a white Angel which used to forbid them what the Devil had bid them do, and told them that those things would not last long. What had been done was permitted because of the Wickedness of the People, and the carrying away of the Children should be made manifest. And they added that this white Angel would place Himself sometimes at the Door betwixt the Witches and the Children, and when they came to Blockula, he pulled the Children back, but the Witches they went in.

Of the Mischief or Evil which the Witches promised to do to Men and Beasts.

They confessed that they were to promise the Devil that they would do all that's Ill, and that the Devil taught them to

---

*In all this hodgepodge of fancy mingled with the practical it is interesting to find here the great dragon cast out in the Book of Revelation.

Milk, which was in this wise. They used to stick a Knife in the Wall and hang a kind of Label on it, which they drew and stroaked, and as long as this lasted the Persons that they had power over were miserably plagued, and the Beasts were milked that way till sometimes they died of it.

A Woman confessed that the Devil gave her a wooden Knife, wherewith, going into Houses, she had power to kill any thing she touched with it. Yet there were few that would confess that they had hurt any Man or Woman.

Being asked whether they had murthered any Children, they confessed that they had indeed tormented many, but did not know whether any of them died of those Plagues. And added that the Devil had shewed them several Places where he had Power to do Mischief.

The Minister of Elfdale declared that one Night these Witches were to his thinking upon the Crown of his Head, and that from thence he had had a long continued Pain of the Head.

One of the Witches confessed too that the Devil had sent her to torment that Minister, and that she was ordered to use a Nail and strike it into his Head, but it would not enter very deep, and thence came that Headache.

The aforesaid Minister said also that one Night he felt a Pain as if he were torn with an Instrument that they cleaned Flax with, or a Flax-comb, and when he waked he heard somebody scratching and scraping at the Window, but could see no-body. And one of the Witches confessed that she was the Person that did it, being sent by the Devil.

The Minister of Mohra declared also that one Night one of these Witches came into his House, and did so violently take him by the Throat that he thought he should have choaked. And waking, he saw the Person that did it, but could not know her, and that for some Weeks he was not able to speak* or perform Divine Service.

An old Woman of Elfdale confessed that the Devil had holpen her to make a Nail which she struck into a Boy's knee, of which Stroke the Boy remained lame a long time. And she

---

*Thus no two sermons a day.

added that before she burnt or was executed by the hand of Justice, the Boy would recover.

They confessed also that the Devil gives them a Beast about the bigness and shape of a young Cat, which they call a Carrier, and that he gives them a Bird too, as big as a Raven, but white. And these two Creatures they can send any where, and wherever they come, they take away all sorts of Victuals they can get, Butter, Cheese, Milk, Bacon, and all sorts of Seeds, whatever they find, and carry it to the Witch. What the Bird brings they may keep for themselves, but what the Carrier brings they must reserve for the Devil, and that's brought to Blockula where he doth give them of it so much as he thinks fit.

They added likewise that these Carriers fill themselves so full sometimes that they are forced to spue by the way, which spueing is found in several Gardens where Colworts grow, and not far from the Houses of those Witches. It is of a yellow colour like Gold, and is called Butter of Witches.

The Lords Commissioners were indeed very earnest, and took great Pains to perswade them to shew some of their Tricks, but to no purpose, for they did all unanimously confess that since they had confessed all they found that all their Witchcraft was gone, and the Devil at this time appeared to them very terribly, with Claws on his Hands and Feet, and with Horns on his Head and long Tail behind, and shewed to them a Pit burning with a Hand put out, but the Devil did thrust the Person down again with an Iron-fork, and suggested to the Witches that if they continued in their Confession he would deal with them in the same manner.

The abovesaid Relation is taken out of the Publick Register, where all this is related with more Circumstances. And at this time through all the Countrey there are Prayers weekly in all Churches, to the end that Almighty God would pull down the Devil's Power, and deliver those poor Creatures which have hitherto groaned under it.

99. The African Chief Condemns His Mother

A chief had lost one of his wives. . . . A little after, the son of one of the other wives, having gone out at midnight, a leopard came upon him and caught his foot fast at the door of the house as he was running in.

The lad was badly bitten, and his mother induced Matope (the chief) to have resort to the usual methods of detecting witchcraft; the result was that his own mother was pronounced a witch. We were very sorry for the poor woman. She lived in another village, over the stream from her son's hamlet. . . . She She was fond of joking and fun, but this sentence made her an object of dread and aversion. Even the natives now shrunk from her; we gave her presents, invited her to come to see us, and cautioned her against drinking the poisoned cup. We made the village chief promise that it would not be administered.

The result was that there was some delay in drinking the ordeal. We made every use of this respite by talking on the matter with Kapéui, the chief of the country, who was her brother, and who promised to use every influence on her behalf. Her son, the chief, was a very successful hunter. During the delay he could not go to hunt. The superstition was too strong for him. At the same time his mother was anxious to break the spell that bound him, she was so sure that she was innocent. She drank the dangerous cup and died, and however dearly the liberty was purchased, the hunter could now go forth to his usual pursuit.

—Duff MacDonald, *Africana*

100. Thirty-one Dead Wives in Africa.

Yesterday there was a procession of the wives of the late son of the king. . .whose death I have already alluded to.

The women came down to the waterside to wash. . . They proceeded to drink poison, from a belief that they had wished their husband's death. . . Out of sixty of these poor, infatuated wretches, thirty-one of them died; while others, who vomited immediately, escaped death.

* * *

(In Calabar) I heard some mournful cries in the bush. . .and approached the place from which the cries proceeded, which was about twenty yards from the waterside on the coast, and I saw there a woman lying chained by a leg to wood, with the arms and legs pinioned, awaiting the period of high water to be launched into the sea, there to become the unhappy prey of voracious sharks. On enquiring. . .I found that she was one of the wives of a chief who had died a few days before, and the brother had selected her for having wished his deceased brother's death.
—M. LAIRD and R. A. K. OLDFIELD,
An Expedition into the Interior of Africa, ii 1837.

101 The Confessions at Paisley

The Tenour of the Confessions taken before Justices at Paisley Assizes Feb. 15, 1678.

As first of Annibal Stuart of the age of fourteen years, or thereby; who declared that she was brought in the presence of the Justices for the crime of Witchcraft; and declared that on Harvest last, the Devil in the shape of a black Man came to her Mother's House, and required the Declarant to give her self up to him; and that the Devil promised her that she should not want any thing that was good.

Declares that she being inticed by her Mother, Jannet Mathie and Bessie Weir who was Officer to their several meetings, she put her hand to the crown of her Head, and the other to the soal of her Foot, and did give herself to the Devil.

Declares that her Mother promised her a new Coat for her doing of it. Declares that her Spirit's Name is Enippa, and that the Devil took her by the Hand and nipped her Arm, which continued to be sore for half an Hour.

Declares that the Devil in the shape of a black Man lay with her in the Bed under the Clothes, and that she found him cold. Declares that thereafter he placed her nearest himself. Declares that she was present in her Mother's House when the Effigies of Wax was made, and that it was made to represent Sir George Maxwel. Declares that the black Man, James Mathie, the Declarant's Mother (whose Spirit's name was Landlady); Bessie Weir, whose Spirit's Name is Sopha, Margaret Craige, whose Spirit's name is Rigerum, and Margaret Jackson, whose Spirit's name is Locas, were all present in the making of the said Effigies, and that they bound it on a Spit and turned it before the Fire, and that it was turned by Bessie Weir, saying as she turned it, "Sir George Maxwel, Sir George Maxwel," and that this was expressed by all of them, and by the Declarant.

Declares that this Picture was made in October last. And further declares that upon the third day of January instant Bessie Weir came to her Mother's House and advertised her to come to her brother John Stuart's the night following.

And that accordingly she came to the place, where she found Bessie Weir, Margery Craige, Margaret Jackson and her Brother John Stuart, and a Man with black Cloths, a blue Band and white Handcuffs with Hogers*, and that his Feet were cloven. And the Declarant sate down by the Fire-side with them, when they made a Picture of Clay, in which they placed Pins in the Breast and sides. And declares that they placed one in every side, and one in the Breast. Declares that the black Man did put Pins in the Picture of Wax, but is not sure who put in the Pins in the Picture of Clay. Declares that the Effigies produced are the Effigies she saw made. Declares that the black Man's name is Ejoall. The Declaration was emitted before James Dunlop of Husil, William Greenlaye, &c. Jan. 27, 1677.

  Ita est.

   ROBERTUS PARK, *Notarius Publicus.*

*High shoes or half boots done up either with laces or buttons.

* * *

The second Confession is of John Stuart, who being interrogate anent this crime of Witchcraft, declared that upon Wednesday the third day of January instant, Bessie Weir in Pollocton came to the Declarant late at night, who being without doors near his own House, the said Bessie Weir did intimate to him that there was a meeting to be at his House the next day. And that the Devil under the shape of a black Man, Margaret Jackson, Margery Craige and the said Bessie Weir were to be present. And that Bessie Weir required the Declarant to be there, which he promised. And that the next night after the Declarant had gone to Bed, the black Man came in and called the Declarant quietly by his name. Upon which he rose from his Bed and put on his Cloths and lighted a Candle. Declares that Margaret Jackson, Bessie Weir and Margery Craige did enter in at a window in the Gavil (gable) of the Declarant's House. And that the first thing the black Man required was that the Declarant should renounce his Baptism and deliver himself up wholly to him. Which the Declarant did by putting one hand on the crown of his Head and the other on the soal of his Foot. And that he was tempted to it by the Devil's promising that he should not want any pleasure, and that he should get his heart filled on all that shall do him wrong.

Declares that he gave him the name of Jonas for his Spirit's name. Declares that thereafter the Devil required every one of their consents for the making of the Effigies of Clay for the taking away the life of Sir George Maxwel of Pollock, to revenge the taking of the Declarant's mother, Uannet Mathie. Declares that every one of the persons above-named gave their consent to the making of the said Effigies, and that they wrought the Clay, and that the black Man did make the Figure of the Head and Face and two Arms to the said Effigies. Declares that the Devil set three Pins in the same, one in each side and one in the Breast, and that the Declarant did hold the Candle to them all the time the Picture was making. And that he observed one of the black Man's Feet to be cloven, and that the black Man's Apparel was black, and that he had a blueish Band and Handcuffs, and that he had Hogers on his Legs without shoes, and that the black Man's Voice was hough (sic) and gousty. And further declares that after they had begun the forming of the Effigies, his Sister Annabil Stuart, a Child of thirteen or fourteen years of Age, came knocking at the Door and being let in by the Declarant, she staid with them a considerable time, but that she went away before the rest, he having opened the Door to her.

Declares that the rest went out at the Window at which they entred. Declares that the Effigies was placed by Bessie Weir in his Bedstraw. He further declares he himself did envy against Sir George Maxwel for apprehending Jannet Mathie, his Mother, and that Bessie Weir had great malice against this Sir George Maxwel, and that her quarrel was, as the Declarant conceived, because the said Sir George had not entered her Husband to his Harvest-service. And also declares that the said Effigies was made upon the fourth day of January instant, and that the Devil's name was Ejoall.

Declares that his Spirits name was Jonas, and Bessie Weir's Spirit's name, who was Officer, was Sopha, and that Margaret Jackson's Spirit's name was Locas, and that Annabil Stuart's, the Declarant's Sisters was Enippa, but does not remember what Margery Craige's Spirits name was. Declares that he cannot write. This Confession was emitted in the presence of the Witnesses to the other Confession, and on the same day.

Ita est.

ROBERTUS PARK, *Notarius Publicus.*

The Confession of Margaret Jackson, Relict of Tho. Stuart in Shaws, who being examined by the Justices anent her being guilty of Witchcraft, declares: that she was present at the making of the first Effigies and Picture that was made in Jannet Mathie's House in October, and that the Devil in the shape of a black Man, Jannet Mathie, Bessie Weir, Margery Craige and Annabil Stuart was present at the making of the said Effigies, and that it was made to represent Sir George Maxwel of Pollock for the taking away his life.

Declares that forty years ago or thereabout, she was at Pollockshawcroft with some few sticks on her back, and that the black Man came to her, and that she did give up her self unto the black Man, and that this was after the Declarant's renouncing of her Baptism, and that the Spirit's name which he designed her, was Locas.

And that about the third or fourth of January instant, or thereby, in the night time when she awaked, she found a Man to be in Bed with her, whom she supposed to have been her Husband, though her Husband had been dead twenty years or thereby, and that the Man immediately disappeared: and declares that this Man who disappeared was the Devil.

Declares that upon Thursday the 4th of January instant, she was present in the House of John Stuart at night when Effigies of Clay was made, and that she saw the black Man there, sometimes sitting, sometimes standing with John Stuart, and that the black Man's Cloths were black, and that he had white Handcuffs. And that Bessie Weir was at Pollockton, and Annabil Stuart in Shaws, and Margery Craige were at the aforesaid time and place of making the said Effigies of Clay, and declares that she gave her consent to the making of the same, and declares that the Devil's name who conspired in the black Man's shape was Ejoall.

Sic subscribitur. Ita Est.
ROBERTUS PARK, *Notarius Publicus, &c.*
—*Saducismus triumphatus*

102. Disease Is Supernatural, in Polynesia

Every disease was supposed to be the effect of direct supernatural agency, and to be inflicted by the gods for some crime against the taboo, of which the sufferer had been guilty, or in consequence of some offering made by an enemy to procure their destruction. Hence, it is probable, in a great measure arises their neglect and cruel treatment of their sick... The natives acknowledged that they possessed articles of poison which, when taken in the food, would procure convulsions and death, but those effects they

considered more the result of the god's displeasure, operating by means of these substitutes, than by the effects of the poisons themselves.
—W. ELLIS, *Polynesian Researches*,iii

103. "God and I Are Equal"

Our big chief, Bulitara, was asking me one day if I had . . .occult powers. When I told him that I made no such claim, he said, "Who makes the wind and the rain and the harvest in your land?"

I answered, "God." "Ah," said he, "that's it. God does this work for your people, and I do it for our people. God and I are equal."

He delivered this dictum very quietly, and with the air of a man who had given a most satisfactory explanation. . . A ruling chief was always supposed to exercise priestly functions, i.e., he professed to be in constant communication with the *tebarans* (spirits), and through their influence he was enabled to bring rain or sickness, fair winds or foul winds, sickness or health, success or disaster in war, and generally to procure any blessing or curse for which the applicant was willing to pay a sufficient price.

REV. GEORGE BROWN, *Melanesians and Polynesians*

* * *

The depositions, the "evidence," and the proceedings in the witchcraft trials that took place in Salem in 1692 fill several volumes, for the vast majority of the relevant documents have been preserved. It is too long and too complicated a story to be repeated here, and only a tiny proportion of the material can be here set down. But the outbreak followed a pattern we have seen illustrated in these pages over and over again—the "possession" of adolescent children, the hysterical accusations of their elders across garden walls, the trials in white frame churches and courthouses wherein the accused were adjudged guilty on evidence we should think nothing but ravings and hallucinations. They were the victims of phenomena they could neither evaluate, nor even understand. We have met Madeleine de la Palüd, whose similar hysteria caused Gauffridi to be burned. We have heard of Loudun and Louviers, enclosed communities where such demoniac possession brought about a brief season of midsummer madness.

Salem was another such community, a secular society this time, but one just as rigidly enclosed and doctrinaire. For an entire year the madness soaked like slow fire in a fuse through almost every part of its body. Then came the inevitable recantations and regret. But seventeenth-century Salem is still so familiar to us that its inhabitants seem almost our neighbors. We know their faces, their voices, their history past and to come in a way we can never know those of seventeenth-century Scots or French or English rustics. They did not suffer the same sort of industrial and agricultural sea change, so Salem people, both victims and accusers, look closer to modern Americans than any seventeenth-century Englishman to his modern equivalent. The Reverend Mr. Burroughs walks down many a main street in Massachusetts, but the Reverend Dr. Glanvill molders away in barely decent obscurity. Greeks and Romans had never turned religion into bigotry. They had never equated godliness with either cleanliness or morality. But the Judaeo-Christian tradition did, and from Sweden to Italy, from the Danube to Massachusetts, the church murdered more people in the name of Christian orthodoxy than any tyrant, or indeed any succession of tyrants has ever done in the name of Empire.

104. John Goodwin's Children in Salem

The first case which I observe was that of four children of a person called John Goodwin, a mason. The eldest, a girl, had quarreled with the laundress of the family about some linen which was missing. The mother of the laundress, an ignorant, testy, and choleric old Irishwoman, scolded the accuser; and shortly after, the elder Goodwin, her sister, and two brothers were seized with such strange diseases, that all their neighbors concluded they were bewitched. They conducted themselves as those supposed to suffer under maladies created by such influence were accustomed to do. They stiffened their necks so hard at one time that the joints could not be moved. At another time their necks were so flexible and supple that it seemed the bone was dissolved. They had violent convulsions, in which their jaws snapped with the force of a spring-trap for vermin. Their limbs were curiously contorted, and to those who had a taste for the marvellous, seemed entirely dislocated and displaced. Amid these distortions, they cried out against the poor old woman, whose name was Glover, alleging that she was in presence with them, adding to their torments.

The miserable Irishwoman, who hardly could speak the English language, repeated her Pater Noster and Ave Maria like a good Catholic; but there were some words which she had forgotten. So she was therefore supposed to be unable to pronounce the whole consistently and correctly—and condemned and executed accordingly.

But the children of Goodwin found the trade they were engaged in too profitable to be laid aside, and the eldest in particular continued all the external signs of witchcraft and possession. Some of these were excellently calculated to flatter the self-opinion and prejudices of the Calvinist ministers by whom she was attended, and accordingly bear in their very front the character of studied and voluntary imposture. The young woman, acting, as was supposed, under the influence of the Devil, read a Quaker treatise with ease and apparent satisfaction; but a book written against the poor inoffensive Friends, the Devil would not allow his victim to touch. She could look on a Church of England Prayer-Book and read the portions of Scripture which it contains without difficulty or impediment; but the spirit which possessed her threw her into fits if she attempted to read the same Scriptures from the Bible, as if the awe which it is supposed the fiends entertain for Holy Writ depended, not on the meaning of the words, but the arrangement of the page and the type in which they were printed. This singular species of flattery was designed to captivate the clergyman through his professional opinion.

—SIR WALTER SCOTT, *Letters on Demonology and Witchcraft*

* * *

[Thus far Sir Walter Scott. Cotton Mather writes of the same case but from an entirely different point of view.]

105. Goody Glover Condemns Herself

It was long before she could with any direct answers plead unto her indictment, and when she did plead it was with confession rather than denial of her guilt. Order was given to search the old woman's house, from whence there were brought into the court several small images, or puppets, or babies, made of rags and stuffed with goat's hair and other such ingredients. When these were produced the old woman acknowledged that her way to torment the objects of her malice was by wetting of her finger with her spittle and stroking of those little images.

The abused children were then present, and the woman still kept stooping and shrinking as one that was almost pressed to death with a mighty weight upon her. But one of the images being brought unto her, immediately she started up after an odd manner and took it into her hand. But she had no sooner taken it than one of the children fell into sad fits before the whole assembly. This the judges had their just apprehensions at, and carefully causing the repetition of the experiment, found again the same event of it. They asked her whether she had any to stand by her. She replied, she had, and looking very pertly in the air she added, "No, he's gone."

And then she confessed that she had one who was her Prince, with whom she maintained I know not what communion. For which cause, the night after, she was heard expostulating with a Devil for his thus deserting her, telling Him that because He had served her so basely and falsely she had confessed all.

However, to make all clear the court appointed five or six physicians one evening to examine her very strictly, whether she were not crazed in her intellectuals and had not procured to herself by folly and madness the reputation of a witch. Diverse hours did they spend with her, and in all that while no discourse came from her but what was pertinent and agreeable. Particularly when they asked her what she thought would become of her soul, she replied, "You ask me a very solemn question, and I cannot well tell what to say to it."

She owned herself a Roman Catholic and could recite her Pater Noster very readily, but there was one clause or two always too hard for her, whereof she said she could not repeat it if she might have all the world. In the upshot the doctors returned her *compos mentis,* and sentence of death was passed upon her.

—COTTON MATHER, *Memorable Providences*

106. Examination of Elizabeth Procter in Salem

"Elizabeth Procter, you understand whereof you are charged, viz., to be guilty of sundry acts of witchcraft; what say you to it? Speak the truth. And so you that are afflicted, you must speak the truth, as you will answer it before god another day. Mary Walcott, doth this woman hurt you?"

"I never saw her so as to be hurt by her."

"Mercy Lewis, does she hurt you?"

Her mouth was stopped.
"Ann Putnam, does she hurt you?"
She could not speak.
"Abigail Williams, does she hurt you?"
Her hand was thrust in her own mouth.
"jOHN (Indian) does this woman hurt you?"
"This is the woman that came in her shift and choked me."
"Did she ever bring the book?"
The Devil's book had to be signed.
"Yes sir."
"What to do?"
"To write."
"What, this woman?"
"Yes sir."
"Are you sure of it?"
"Yes sir."

Again Abigail Williams and Ann Putnam were spoke to by the court, but neither of them could make any answer, by reason of dumbness or other fits.

"What do you say, Goody Procter, to these things?"
"I take God in heaven to be my witness that I know nothing it, no more than the child unborn."

Joseph Bailey testifies.

When I came in sight of the house where John Procter did live there was a very hard blow struck on my breast which caused great pain in my stomach and amazement in my head. But I did see no person near me, only my wife behind me on the same horse. And when I came against said Procter's house, according to my understanding I did see John Procter and his wife at said house. Procter himself looked out of the window and his wife did stand just without the door. I told my wife of it, and she did look that way and could see nothing but a little maid at the door. I saw no maid there, but Procter's wife according to my understanding did stand at the door.

Afterwards, about a mile from the aforesaid house, I was taken speechless for some short time. My wife did ask me several questions, and desired me that if I could not speak I should hold up my hand, which I did. And immediately I could speak as well as ever. And when we came to the way where Salem Road cometh into Ipswich Road, there I received another blow on my breast which caused much pain, that I could not sit on my horse. And when I did alight off my horse, to my understanding I saw a woman coming towards us about sixteen or twenty pole from us, but did not know who it was. My wife could not see her. When I did get up on my horse again, to my understanding there stood a cow where I saw the woman. After that we went to Boston without any further molestation, but after I came home again to Newbury I was pinched and nipped by something invisible for some time. But now through God's goodness to me, I am well again.

* * *

The testimony of William Raymond, aged twenty-six years or thereabout, testifyeth and saith that I being at the house of Lieutenant Ingersoll some time in the latter end of March, there discoursing concerning the examining of several persons suspected for witches, I was saying that I heard that Goody Procter was to be examined tomorrow, to which Goody Ingersoll replied she did not believe it, for she heard nothing of it. Some of the afflicted persons being present, one of them or more cried out, "There, Goody Procter, there, Goody Procter," and "Old Witch, I'll have her hang." Goody Ingersoll sharply reproved them. They seemed to make a joke of it.

* * *

The Testimony of Daniel Eliot, aged twenty-seven or thereabouts, who testifieth and saith, that I being at the house of Lieutenant Ingersoll on the 28th of March in the year 1692, there being present one of the afflicted persons, which cried out and said, "There's Goody Procter," William Raymond being there present told the girl he believed she lied, for he saw nothing. Goody Ingersoll told the girl she told a lie. Then the girl said she did it for sport—they must have some sport.
—*Records of Salem Witchcraft,* Rosbury, Mass., 1864

107. An Appeal from Salem Prison

Salem Prison,
July 23, '92.

Mr Mather, Mr Allen, Mr Moody, Mr Willard and Mr Bailey.
Reverend Gentlemen,

The innocency of our case, with the enmity of our accusers and our judges and jury, whom nothing but our innocent blood will serve their turn, having condemned us already before our trials, being so much incensed and encouraged against us by the Devil, makes us bold to beg and implore your favourable assistance of this our humble petition to his Excellency, that if it be possible our innocent blood may be spared, which undoubtedly otherwise will be shed if the Lord doth not mercifully step in, the magistrates, ministers, juries and all the people in general being so much enraged and incensed against us by the delusion of the Devil, which we can term no other, by reason we know in our own consciences we are all innocent persons. Here are five people who have lately confessed themselves to be witches and do accuse some of us of being along with them at a Sacrament since we were committed into close prison, which we know to be lies. Two of the five are young men who would not confess anything till they tied them neck and heels till the blood was ready to come out of their noses. And 'tis credibly believed and reported this was the occasion of making them confess that they never did, by reason they said one had been a witch a month and another five weeks, and that their mother had made them so, who has been confined here nine weeks.

My son, William Procter, when he was examined, because he would not confess that he was guilty when he was innocent, they tied him neck and heels till the blood gushed out at his nose, and would have kept him so twenty-four hours if one more merciful than the rest had not taken pity on him and caused him to be unbound.

These actions are very like the Popish cruelties. They have already undone us in our estates, and that will not serve their turn without our innocent blood. If it cannot be granted that we can have our trials at Boston, we humbly beg that you would endeavor to have these magistrates changed and others in their rooms, begging also and beseeching you would be pleased to be here, if not all, some of you at our trials, hoping thereby you may be the means of saving the shedding of innocent blood, desiring your prayers to the Lord in our behalf, we rest your poor afflicted servants,

John Procter, etc.

Procter's appeal fell on deaf ears. He and his companions were hanged on the 19th of August.

They protested their innocency as in the presence of the great God whom forthwith they were to appear before. They wished, and declared their wish, that their blood might be the last innocent blood shed upon that account. With great affection they entreated Mr C M (Cotton Mather) to pray with them. They prayed that God would discover what witchcrafts were among us. They forgave their accusers. They spake without reflection on jury and judges for bringing them in guilty and condemning them. They prayed earnestly for pardon for all other sins and for an interest in the precious blood of our dear Redeemer, and seemed to be very sincere, upright and sensible of their circumstances on all accounts, especially Procter and Willard, whose whole management of themselves from the jail to the gallows and whilst at the gallows was very affecting and melting to the hearts of some considerable spectators.

—ROBERT CALEF, *More Wonders of the Invisible World*

108. Testimony Against Bridget Bishop

Richard Coman testifies:

I being awake did then see Bridget Bishop of Salem, alias Oliver, come into the room we lay in and two women more with her, which two women were strangers to me. I knew them not, but said Bishop came in her red paragon bodice and the rest of her clothing which she then usually did wear . . . And quickly after they appeared the light was out, and the curtains at the foot of the bed opened, where I did see her.

And presently (she) came and lay upon my breast or body and so oppressed me that I could not speak or stir, no not so much as to awake my wife, although I endeavored much so to do it. The next night they all appeared again in like manner, and the said Bishop, alias Oliver, took hold of me by the throat and almost hauled me out of the bed. The Saturday night following, I having been that day telling of what I had seen and how I suffered the two nights before, my kinsman William Coman told me he would stay with me and lodge with me and see if they would come agian, and advised me to lay my sword athwart my body. Quickly after we went to bed that same night, and both well awake and discoursing together, in came all the three women again, and said Bishop was the first as she had been the other two nights.

So I told him, "William, here they be all come again." And he was immediately struck speechless and could not move hand or foot. And immediately they got hold of my sword and strived to take it from me, but I held so fast as they did not get it away. And I then had liberty of speech and called William, also my wife, and Sarah Phillips that lay with my wife, who all told me afterwards they heard me but had not power to speak or stir . . .

And the first that spake was Sarah Phillips, and said, "In the name of God, Goodman Coman, what is the matter with you?" So they all vanished away.

Samuel Gray deposes that he saw:
a woman standing between the cradle in the room and the bedside and seemed to look upon him. So he did rise up in his bed and it vanished . . . Then he went to the door and found it locked. And unlocking and opening the door he went to the entry door and looked out, and then again did see the same woman he had a little before seen in the room, and in the same garb she was in before. Then he said to her, "In the name of God, what do you come for?" Then she

vanished away. So he locked the door again and went to bed. And between sleeping and waking he felt something come to his lips, cold, and thereupon started and looked up, and again did see the same woman with something between her hands, holding before his mouth. Upon which she moved, and the child in the cradle gave a great screech out, as if it was greatly hurt, and she disappeared.

And taking the child up, (he) could not quiet it in some hours. From which time the child, that before was a very likely thriving child, did pine away and was never well (although it lived some months after, yet in a sad condition) and so died.

Some time after, within a week or less, he did see the same woman in the same garb or clothes that appeared to him as aforesaid . . . although he knew not her nor her name before. Yet both by her garb and countenance (he) doth testify that it was the same woman that they now call Bridget Bishop, alias Oliver, of Salem.

John Louder deposes:

About seven or eight years since, I then living with Mr John Gedney in Salem . . . had some controversy with Bridget Bishop, the wife of Edward Bishop of Salem, sawyer, about her fowls that used to come into our orchard or garden. Some little time after which, I going well to bed, about the middle of the night felt a great weight upon my breast, and awakening, looked, and it being bright moonlight, did clearly see Bridget Bishop or her likeness sitting upon my stomach. And putting my arms off of the bed to free myself from that great oppression, she presently laid hold of my throat and almost choked me, and I had no strength or power in my hands to resist or help myself. And in this condition she held me to almost day.

Some time after this my mistress, Susannah Gedney, was in our orchard and I was then with her, and said Bridget Bishop being then in her orchard which was next adjoining to ours, my mistress told said Bridget that I said or affirmed that she came one night and sat upon my breast as aforesaid, which she denied and I affirmed to her face to be true, and that I did plainly see her, upon which discourse with her she threatened me. And some time after that, I not being very well, stayed at home on a Lord's Day. And on the afternoon of said day, the doors being shut, I did see a black pig in the room coming towards me. So I went towards it to kick it and it vanished away. Immediately after, I sat down . . . and did see a black thing jump into the window. And (it) came and stood just before my face . . . The body of it looked like a monkey, only the feet were like a cock's feet with claws, and the face somewhat more like a man's than a monkey's. And I being greatly affrighted, not being able to speak or help myself by reason of fear, I suppose, so the thing spoke to me and said, "I am a messenger sent to you. For I understand you are troubled in mind, and if you will be ruled by me you shall want for nothing in this world."

Upon which I endeavored to clap my hands upon it, and said, "You Devil, I will kill you," but could feel no substance. And it jumped out of the window again and immediately came in by the porch, although the doors were shut, and said, "You had better take my counsel."

Whereupon I struck at it with a stick, but struck the groundsill and broke the stick, but felt no substance, and that arm with which I struck was presently disenabled. Then it vanished away and I opened the back door and went out, and going towards the house end I espied said Bridget Bishop in her orchard going towards her house, and seeing her, had no power to set one foot forward, but returned in again. And going to shut the door, I again did see that or the like creature that I before did see within doors, in such a posture as it seemed to be going to fly at me.

Upon which I cried out, "The whole armor of God . . . be between me and you?" So it sprang back and flew over the apple tree, flinging the dust with its feet against my stomach, upon which I was struck dumb and so continued for about three days time. And also shook many of the apples off from the tree which it flew over.
—COTTON MATHER, *Wonders of the Invisible World* and *Records of Salem Witchcraft*, Roxbury, Massachusetts, 2 vols., 1864

* * *

But Bridget Bishop denied knowing John Louder, though they lived next door to each other. They found puppets made of rags and hogs' bristles in the wall of her house. There was a rumor current that she had bewitched her first husband, one Wasslebee, and during her second marriage she had actually been brought to trial for witchcraft and acquitted. Her third husband, Edward Bishop, had accused her of "sitting up all night with the Devil," and that, with the evidence of Gray, Coman, and Louder, was enough. She was sentenced to be hanged.

109. Death Warrant of Bridget Bishop

To George Corwin, Gentm. high Shireffe of the County of Essex Greeting.

Whereas Bridgett Bishop alias Oliver, the wife of Edward Bishop of Salem in the County of Essex, Sawyer, at a speciall court of Oyer and Terminer held at Salem the second Day of this instant month 4th of June for the Countyes of Essex, Middlesex and Suffolk before William Stoughton Esqr. and his Associate Justices of the said Court was Indicted and arraigned upon five severall Indictments for useing practising and exercising on the nyneteenth day of April last and divers other dayes and times before and after, certain acts of Witchcraft upon the bodyes of Abigail Williams, Ann Puttnam Junr, Mercy Lewis, Mary Walcott and Elizabeth Hubbard of Salem Village, Singlewomen, whereby their bodyes were hurt, afflicted, pined, consumed, Wasted and tormented, contrary to the forme of the Statute in that Case made and provided.

To which Indictments the said Bridgett Bishop pleaded not guilty and for tryall thereof put herself upon God and her Country, whereupon she was found guilty of the felonys and witchcrafts whereof she stood Indicted and sentence of Death accordingly passed against her as the Law directs.

Execution whereof yet remains to be done.

These are therefore in the name of their Majesties William

and Mary now King and Queen over England &c to will and Command you that upon Fryday next being the Tenth day of this instant month of June between the hours of Eight and Twelve in the aforenoon of the same day you safely conduct the said Bridget Bishop alias Oliver from their Majesties Goal (sic) in Salem aforesaid to the place of Execution and there cause her to be hanged by the neck until she be dead, and of your doings herein make return to the Clerke of the said Court.

And hereof you are not to faile at your peril.

And this shall be your sufficient Warrant. Given under my hand and seal at Boston the Eighth day of June in the fourth year of the Reign of our Sovereign Lord and Lady William and Mary, now King and Queen over England, 8c. Anno Dom 1692

Wm. Stoughton.

June 10th 1692.

According to the within Written precept, I have taken the body of the within named Bridgett Bishop out of their Majesties Goale in Salem and Safely Conveighed her to the place provided for her Execution and caused the said Bridgett to be hanged by the neck untill shee was dead, all which was according to the time within Required, and so I make Returne by me.

George Corwin, Sheriff.
—Records of Salem Witchcraft

110. From the Examination of George Jacobs

Doth he ever pray in his family?
Not unless by himself.
Why do you not pray in your family?
I cannot read.

—Records of Salem Witchcraft

* * *

Sarah Good was another victim. "A melancholy and distracted woman," she was called. She had a child of four or five, a girl called Dorcas. And even young Dorcas testified against her.

111. From the Examination of Sarah Good

JUDGE HATHORNE: Sarah Good, what evil Spirit have you familiarity with?
GOOD: None.
HATHORNE: Have you made no contracts with the devil?
GOOD: No.
HATHORNE: Why doe you hurt these children?
GOOD: I doe not hurt them. I scorn it.
HATHORNE: Who doe you imploy then to hurt them?
GOOD: I imploy nobody.
HATHORNE: What creature do you imploy then?
GOOD: No creature. But I am falsely accused.
HATHORNE: Why did you go away muttering from Mr. Parris his house?
GOOD: I did not mutter. But I thanked him for what he gave my child.
HATHORNE: Have you made no contract with the devil?
GOOD: No.
Mr. Hathorne desired the children all of them to look upon her and see if this were the person what had hurt them, and so they all did looke upon her, and said this was one of the persons that did torment them—presently they were all tormented.
HATHORNE: Sarah Good, do you not see now what you have done? Why doe you not tell us the truth? Why doe you thus torment these poor children?
GOOD: I doe not torment them.
HATHORNE: Who doe you imploy then?

Good: I imploy nobody. I scorn it.
Hathorne: How came they thus tormented?
Good: What doe I know? You bring others here and now you charge me with it.
Hathorne: Why, who was it?
Good: I do not know. But it was some you brought into this meeting house with you.
Hathorne: We brought you into the meeting house.
Good: But you brought in two more.
Hathorne: Who was it then that tormented the children?
Good: It was Osburn.
Hathorne: What is it you say when you go muttering away from peoples houses?
Good: If I must tell, I will tell.
Hathorne: Doe tell us then.
Good: If I must tell, I will tell. It is the commandments. I may say my commandments, I hope.
Hathorne: What commandment is it?
Good: If I must tell, I will tell. It is a psalm.
Hathorne: What psalm?
Good: (After a time she muttered over some parts of a psalm.)
Hathorne: Who doe you serve?
Good: I serve God.
Hathorne: What God doe you serve?
Good: The God that made heaven and earth. (Though she was not willing to mention the word God.) Her answers were in a very wicked, spiteful manner, reflecting and retorting against the authority with base and abussive words and many lies she was taken in. It was here said that her husband had said that he was afraid that she was either a witch or would be one very quickly. The worshipful Mr Hathorne asked him his reason why he said so of her, whether he had ever seen any thing by her. He answered no, not in this nature, but it was her bad carriage to him, and indeed, said he, I may say with tears that she is an enemy of all good.

       Salem Village, March the 1st, 1691.
       Written by Ezekiell Chevers.
       —*Records of Salem Witchcraft*

* * *

On the 19th of July she was hanged along with four others. But even at the end her waspish temperament did not desert her. The Reverend Mr. Noyes called on her to confess that she was a witch. Twenty-five years later when he himself died, the people of Salem still remembered her reply as the executioner tied the rope round her neck:

GOOD: You are a liar. I am no more a witch than you are a wizard, and if you take away my life God will give you blood to drink.

The Reverend Nicholas Noyes was drowned with a rush of blood to his throat.

112. Nathaniel Cary Attends His Wife's Hearing

Captain Nathaniel Cary of Charlestown writes:
I having heard some days that my wife was accused of witchcraft, being much disturbed by it, by advice we went to Salem Village to see if the afflicted did know her. We arrived there 24 May; it happened to be a day appointed for examination.

Accordingly, soon after our arrival Mr Hathorn and Mr Corwin, etc., went to the Meeting-House which was the place appointed for that work. The minister began with prayer. And having taken care to get a convenient place, I observed that the afflicted were two girls of about ten years old, and about two or three others of about eighteen. One of the girls talked most, and could discern more than the rest.

The prisoners were called in one by one and as they came in were cried out of, etc. The prisoner was placed about seven or eight foot from the justices and the accusers between the justices and them. The prisoner was ordered to stand right before the justices, with an officer appointed to hold each hand lest they should therewith afflict them. And the prisoner's eye must be constantly on the justices, for if they looked on the afflicted they would either fall into their fits or cry out of being hurt by them.

After examination of the prisoners who it was afflicted these girls, etc., they were put upon saying the Lord's Prayer as a trial of their guilt. After the afflicted seemed to be out of their fits they would look steadfastly on some one person, and frequently not speak (and then the justices said they were struck dumb), and after a little time would speak again.

Then the justices said to the accusers, "Which of you will go and touch the prisoner at the bar?" Then the most courageous would adventure, but before they had made three steps would ordinarily fall down, as in a fit. The justices ordered that they should be taken up and carried to the prisoner, that she might touch them. And as soon as they were touched by the accused the justices would say, "They are well," before I could discern any alteration, by which I observed that the justices understood the manner of it. Thus far I was only a spectator. My wife also was there part of the time, but no notice was taken of her by the afflicted except once or twice they came to her and asked her name.

But I having an opportunity to discourse Mr Hale (with whom I had formerly acquaintance), I took his advice what I had best to do, and desired of him that I might have an opportunity to speak with her that accused my wife, which he promised should be, I acquainting him that I reposed my trust in him.

Accordingly he came to me after the examination was over and told me I had now an opportunity to speak with the said accuser, viz. Abigail Williams, a girl of eleven or twelve years old but that we would not be in private at Mr Parris' house as he had promised me.

We went therefore into the ale house, where an Indian man attended us who it seems was one of the afflicted. To him we gave some cider. He showed several scars that seemed as if they had been long there, and showed them as done by witchcraft, and acquainted us that his wife, who also was a slave, was imprisoned for witchcraft. And now instead of one accuser they all came in, who began to tumble down like swine, and then three women were called in to attend them. We in the room were all at a stand to see who they would cry out of, but in a short time they cried out, "Cary." And immediately after a warrant was sent from the justices to bring my wife before them, who were sitting in a chamber nearby waiting for this.

Being brought before the justices, her chief accusers were two girls. My wife declared to the justices that she never had any knowledge of them before that day. She was forced to stand with her arms stretched out. I did request that I might hold one of her hands, but it was denied me; then she desired me to wipe the tears from her eyes and the sweat from her face, which I did; then she desired she should lean herself on me, saying she should faint.

Justice Hathorne replied, she had strength enough to torment those persons and she should have strength enough to stand. I speaking something against their cruel proceedings, they commanded me to be silent or else I should be turned out of the room. The Indian before mentioned was also brought in to be one of her accusers. Being come in, he now (when before the justices) fell down and tumbled about like a hog, but said nothing.

The justices asked the girls who afflicted the Indian. They answered "She," (meaning my wife) and now lay upon him. The justices ordered her to touch him, in order to his cure, but her head must be turned another way lest instead of curing she should make him worse by her looking on him, her hand being guided to take hold of his. But the Indian took hold on her hand and pulled her down on the floor in a barbarous manner. Then his hand was taken off and her hand put on his and the cure was quickly wrought. I being extremely troubled at their inhumane dealings uttered a hasty speech (that God would take vengeance on them, and desired that God would deliver us out of the hands of unmerciful men).

Then her *Mittimus* was writ. I did with difficulty and charge obtain the liberty of a room, but no beds in it. If there had (been), could have taken but little rest that night. She was committed to Boston Prison, but I obtained a *Habeus Corpus* to remove her to Cambridge Prison, which is in our

County of Middlesex. Having been there one night, next morning the jailer put irons on her legs (having received such a command). The weight of them was about eight pounds. These irons and her other afflictions soon brought her into convulsion fits, so that I thought she would have died that night. I sent to entreat that the irons might be taken off, but all entreaties were in vain if it would have saved her life, so that in this condition she must continue.
—ROBERT CALEF, *More Wonders of the Invisible World*

* * *

On the 30th of July Captain Cary managed to help his wife to escape out of prison, and he fled with her to New York.

Giles Corey, on the other hand, knew something that "would do his wife's business." She too "afflicted" young girls, however, so Edward Putnam and Ezekiel Cheever decided to go and see her.

113. Ann Putnam and Goody Corey

We Desired Ann Putnam to take good notice of what clothes Goody Corey (i.e., her spirit) came in, that so we might see whether she was not mistaken in the person. And accordingly we went to the house of Thomas Putnam before we went to Goody Corey to see what Ann would say about her clothes, and she told us that presently after we had told her that we would go and talk with Goody Corey she came and blinded her, but told her that her name was Corey and that she should see her no more before it was night, and then she would come again and pay her off. Then we went both of us away from the home of Thomas Putnam to the house of Giles Corey . . .

And as soon as we came in, in a smiling manner she saith,

"I know what you are come for; you are come to talk with me about being a witch, but I am none. I cannot help people's talking of me."

Edward Putnam answered her that it was the afflicted person that did complain of her that was the occasion of our coming to her.

She presently replied, "But does she tell you what clothes I have on?"

We made her no answer to this at her first asking, whereupon she asked again with very great eagerness, "But does she tell you what clothes I have on?"

Which questions, with that eagerness of mind with which she did ask, made us to think of what Ann Putnam had told us before we went to her, and we told her no, she did not, for she told us that you came and blinded her and told her that she should see you no more before it was night, that so she might not tell us what clothes you had on. She made but little answer to this but seemed to smile at it, as if she had showed us a pretty trick.

> *It is a matter of some interest that Ann Putnam was twelve years old at the time, and even though Martha Corey was no hysterical old woman, but an intelligent and somewhat righteous churchgoer, she was subjected to a particularly brutal cross-examination by Justice Hathorne, convicted and sentenced to be hanged. On the 22nd of September she was executed. But a week before, her eighty-year-old husband, who had at first accused her, was himself brought to trial. On the 16th of September:*

Giles Corey pleaded not guilty to his indictment, but would not put himself upon Tryall by the Jury (they having cleared none upon Tryall) and knowing that there would be the same Witnesses against him, rather chose to undergo what Death they should put him to. In pressing, his Tongue being prest out of his mouth, and the Sheriff with his Cane forced it in again, when he was dying. He was the first in New England that was ever prest to death.

—*Records of Salem Witchcraft*

* * *

Twelve-year-old Ann Putnam was indefatigable.

114. The Deposition of Ann Putnam

Who testifieth and saith that on 20th of April, 1692 at evening she saw the Apparishton of a minister at which she was grieviously affrighted and cried out oh dreadfull: dreadfull her is a minister com, what are Ministers wicthes to: whence com you and What is your name for I will complaine of you tho you be a Minister: if you be a wizzard.

> *One cannot help interrupting to mention that Ann Putnam's deposition is here set down precisely as it was written. I have not always copied the wilder flights of orthography, but here for once I am letting the witness speak in her own voice, a voice which in this case brought a clergyman to the gallows.*

and Immediately I was tortored by him being Racked and allmost choaked by him: and he tempted me to write in his book which I Refused with loud out cries and said I would not writ in his book tho he tore me al to peaces but tould him that it was a dreadfull thing: that he which was a Minister that should teach children to feare God should com to perswad poor creatures to give their souls to the devill; oh, dreadfull, dreadfull, tell me your name that I may know who you are; then againe he tortored me and urged me to writ in his book; which I refused and then presently he tould me that his name was George Burroughs, and that he had had three wives: and that he had bewicthed the Two first of them to death; and that he had kiled Miss T. Lawson because she was so unwilling to goe from the village, and also killed Mr Lawson's child because he went to the eastward with Sir

Edmon and preached to the souldiers and that he had made Abigail Hobbs a wicth and several wicthes more: and he has continwed ever sence; by times tempting me to write in his book and grievously tortoring me by beating, pinching and almost choaking me severall times a day and he also tould me that he was above a wicth he was a conjuror.

On the 3rd of May she adds: Then immediately appeared to me the forme of two women in winding-sheats, and napkins about their heads, att which I was grately affrighted. And they turned their faces towards Mr Burroughs and looked very red and angury and tould him that he had been a cruell man to them, and that their blood did crie for vengeance against him and also tould him that they should be cloathed with white Robes in heaven when he would be cast into hell. And immediately he vanished away. And as soon as he was gon the Two women turned their faces towards me and looked as pail as a white wall, and tould me that they were Mr Burroughs' Two first wives and that he had murthered them. And one tould me that she was his first wife, and he stabed her under the left Arme and put a peece of sealing wax on the wound. And she pulled aside the winding-sheat and showed me the place, and also tould me that she was in the house Mr. Parris now lived where it was don. And the other tould me that Mr Burroughs and that wife which he now hath kiled her on the vessell as she was coming to see her friends, because they would have one another, and they both charged me that I should tell these things to the Magistrates before Mr Burroughs face and if he did not own them they did not know but they should appere there: thes morning. Also Mis Lawson and hir daughter Ann appeared to me whom I knew, and tould me that Mr Burroughs murthered them; this morning also appered to me another woman in a winding sheet and tould me that she was Goodman ffulers first wife and Mr. Burroughs killed her because there was sum difference between hir husband and him.

> Burroughs appeared to Susannah Sheldon, too and volunteered the information that he had murdered two of his wives, and no one seems to have considered it odd that a man should appear to young girls in order to inform them that he

was a murderer, and then should identify himself so that he could more easily be apprehended. But then Burroughs seems to have been a remarkable man. Though comparatively slightly built, he could lift a barrel of molasses by thrusting two fingers into the bunghole, and one witness reported that he had held a seven-foot fowling piece out at arm's length on a forefinger stuck into the muzzle. In addition, he boasted of possessing powers of clairvoyance. He had once alarmed his wife by telling her what she had talked about while he was away. His brother-in-law, Goodman Ruck, reported a similar story. It seems that he, his sister, and Mr. Burroughs were one day gathering strawberries. What followed puzzled him hugely.

Burroughs stepped aside a little into the bushes, whereupon they halted and halooed for him. He not answering, they went away homewards with a quickened pace without any expectation of seeing him in a considerable while. And yet when they were got near home, to their astonishment they found him on foot with them, having a basket of strawberries. (He) immediately then fell to chiding his wife on the account of what she had been speaking to her brother on the road, which, when they had wondered at, he said he knew their thoughts. Ruck being startled at that, made some reply intimating that the Devil himself did not know so far. But (Burroughs) answered, "My God makes known your thoughts unto me."

For some unimaginable reason Burroughs allowed himself to be caught telling flagrant lies in the dock, and that alone was almost enough to convict him. In any case, convicted he was, and on the 19th of August he was brought out with several others to be hanged.

Mr Burroughs was carried in a cart with the others through the streets of Salem to execution. When he was upon the ladder he made a speech for the clearing of his innocency, with such solemn and serious expressions as were to the admiration of all present. His prayer (which he concluded by repeating the Lord's prayer) was so well worded, and uttered with such composedness, and such (at least seeming) fervency of spirit as was very affecting and drew tears from many (so that it seemed to some that the spectators would hinder the execution). (But) when he was cut down he was dragged by the halter to a hole, or grave, between the rocks, about two feet deep, his shirt and breeches being pulled off and an old pair of trousers of one executed put on his lower parts. He was put in, together with Willard and Carrier, one of his hands and his chin and a foot of one of them being left uncovered.

—*Records of Salem Witchcraft*

115. The Deposition of Sarah Ingersoll

The deposition of Sarah Ingersoll, aged about thirty years, saith that seeing Sarah Churchill after her examination, she came to me crying and wringing her hands, seeming to be much troubled in spirit. I asked her what she ailed. She answered, she had undone herself. I asked her in what. She said in belying herself and others, in saying she had set her hand to the Devil's book, whereas she said she never did. I told her I believed she had set her hand to the book. She answered crying, and said, "No, no, no. I never, I never did."

I asked then what made her say she did. She answered because they threatened her and told her they would put her into the dungeon, and put her along with Mr Burroughs. And thus several times she followed me up and down, telling me that she had undone herself in belying herself and others. I asked her why she did not write it. She told me, because she had stood out so long in it that now she durst not. She said also that if she told Mr Noyes but once she had set her hand to the book, he would believe her, but if she told the truth and said she had not set her hand to the book a hundred times he would not believe her.

—*Records of Salem Witchcraft*

116. Goody Tyler's Evidence to Increase Mather

19th October.

Goodwife Tyler did say that when she was first apprehended she had no fears upon her and did think that nothing could have made her confess against herself. But since, she had found to her great grief that she had wronged the truth and falsely accused herself. She said that when she was brought to Salem her brother Bridges rode with her, and that all along the way from Andover to Salem her brother kept telling her that she must needs be a witch, since the afflicted accused her and at her touch were raised out of their fits, and urging her to confess herself a witch.

She as constantly told him that she was no witch, that she knew nothing of witchcraft, and begged of him not to urge her to confess. However, when she came to Salem she was carried to a room where her brother on one side and Mr John Emerson on the other side did tell her that she was certainly a witch, and that she saw the Devil before her eyes at that time (and accordingly the said Emerson would attempt with his hand to beat him away from her eyes), and they so urged her to confess that she wished herself in any dungeon rather than be so treated.

Mr. Emerson told her once and again, "Well, I see you will not confess. Well! I will now leave you, and then you are undone body and soul forever."

Her brother urged her to confess and told her that in so doing she could not lie, to which she answered, "Good brother, do not say so. For I shall lie if I confess, and then who shall answer unto God for my lie?"

He still asserted it, and said that God would not suffer so many good men to be in such an error about it, and that she would be hanged if she would not confess, and continued so long and so violently to urge and press her to confess that she thought verily her life would have gone from her, and became so terrified in her mind that she owned at length almost anything that they propounded to her. But she had wronged her conscience in so doing; she was guilty of a great sin in belying of herself, and desired to mourn for it as long as she lived. This she said and a great deal more of the like nature, and all of it with such affection, sorrow, relenting, grief and mourning, as that it exceeds any pen for to describe and express the same.

—*Massachusetts Historical Society Collections*

* * *

One of the victims who was so patently innocent that even the redoubtable Justice Hathorne had his doubts. She was even released, but shortly thereafter the fits of one of the afflicted girls so increased in severity that she had to be rearrested. This time she was condemned to death, and on the 22nd of September she was hanged. But shortly before her execution, she wrote the following letter from her cell.

117. Mary Easty's Appeal Before Hanging

To the honourable Judge and Bench now sitting in judicature in Salem and the Reverend Ministers, humbly sheweth that whereas your humble poor Petitioner being condemned to die doth humbly beg of you to take it into your Judicious and Pious Considerations that your poor and humble Petitioner, knowing my own Innocency (blessed be the Lord for it) and seeing plainly the Wiles and Subtilty of my accusers by myself, cannot but judge charitably of others that are going the same way with myself if the Lord step not mightily in.

I was confined a whole Month on the same account that I am now condemned for, and then cleared by the Afflicted persons, as some of your Honours know. And in two days time I was cried out upon by them, and have been confined and now am condemned to die.

The Lord above knows my Innocency then and likewise doth now, as at the Great Day will be known to Men and

Angels. I Petition to your Honours not for my own Life, for I know I must die, and my appointed time is set. But the Lord he knows it is, if it be possible, that no more Innocent Blood be shed, which undoubtedly cannot be avoided in the way and course you go in.

I question not but your Honours do the utmost of your powers in the discovery and detecting of Witchcraft and Witches, and would not be guilty of Innocent Blood for the world. But by my own Innocency I know you are in the wrong way. The Lord in his infinite Mercy direct you in this great work, if it be His blessed will that Innocent Blood be not shed.

I would humbly beg of you that your Honours would be pleased to Examine some of those confessing Witches, I being confident there are several of them have belied themselves and others, as will appear, if not in this World, I am sure in the World to come whither I am going. And I question not but yourselves will see an alteration in these things.

They say myself and others have made a league with the Devil; we cannot confess. I know and the Lord he knows (as will shortly appear) they belye me, and so I question not but they do others. The Lord alone, who is the searcher of all hearts, knows that as I shall answer it at the Tribunal Seat that I know not the least thing of Witchcraft, wherefore I cannot, I durst not belye my own Soul. I beg your Honours not to deny this my humble Petition from a poor dying Innocent person, and I question not but the Lord will give a blessing to your endeavours.

MARY EASTY
—More Wonders of the Invisible World

118. The Hearing of John Alden, Mariner

John Alden, Senior, of Boston in the County of Suffolk, Mariner, on the 28th day of May, 1692 was sent for by the

Magistrates of Salem, in the County of Essex, upon the accusation of a company of poor distracted or possessed creatures, or witches, and being sent by Mr Stoughton arrived there on the 31st of May and appeared at Salem Village before Mr Gedney, Mr Hathorne, and Mr. Corwin.

Those wenches being present, who played their juggling tricks, falling down, crying out and staring in people's faces, the Magistrates demanded of them several times who it was of all the people in the room that hurt them. One of these accusers pointed several times at one Captain Hill, there present, but spake nothing. The same accuser had a man standing at her back to hold her up; he stooped down to her ear; then she cried out Alden, Alden afflicted her. One of the Magistrates asked her if she had ever seen Alden. She answered, no. He asked her how she knew it was Alden. She said, the man told her so.

Then all were ordered to go down into the street, where a ring was made and the same accuser cried out, "There stands Alden, a bold fellow with a hat on before the Judges. He sells powder and shot to the Indians and French, and lies with the Indian squaws and has Indian papooses."

Then was Alden committed to the Marshall's custody and his sword taken from him, for they said he afflicted them with his sword. After some hours Alden was sent for to the Meeting House in the Village before the Magistrates, who required Alden to stand upon a chair, to the open view of all the people.

The accusers cried out that Alden did pinch them then, when he stood upon a chair in the sight of all the people, a good way distant from them. One of the Magistrates bid the Marshall to hold open Alden's hands, that he might not pinch those creatures.

Alden asked them why they should think that he should come to that Village to afflict those persons that he never knew or saw before. Mr Gedney bid Alden confess and give glory to God. Alden said he hoped he should give glory to God and hoped he should never gratify the Devil, but appealed to all that ever knew him if they ever suspected him to be such a person, and challenged anyone that could bring in anything upon their own knowledge that might give suspicion of his being such an one.

Mr Gedney said he had known Alden many years, and had been at sea with him, and always looked upon him to be an honest man, but now he did see cause to alter his judgement. Alden answered, he was sorry for that, but he hoped God would clear up his innocency that he would recall that judgement again, and added that he hoped that he should with Job maintain his integrity till he died.

They bid Alden look upon the accusers, which he did, and then they fell down. Alden asked Mr Gedney what reason there could be given why Alden's looking upon *him* should not strike *him* down as well, but no reason was given that I heard. But the accusers were brought to Alden to touch them, and this touch they said made them well. Alden began to speak of the Providence of God in suffering these creatures to accuse innocent persons. Mr Noyes asked Alden why he would offer to speak of the Providence of God. "God by His Providence," said Mr Noyes, "governs the world and keeps it in peace," and so went on with discourse and stopped Alden's mouth as to that. Alden told Mr Gedney that he could assure them that there was a lying spirit in them, "For I can assure you that there is not a word of truth in all these say to me." But Alden was again committed to the Marshall, and his *Mittimus* written.

—*More Wonders of the Invisible World*

* * *

Alden was eventually freed. And, in any case, by the turn of the year the fire had burned itself out. Not that the "fits" ceased altogether. Cotton Mather reports one such afflicted girl who went so far as to suggest that he, himself, might be guilty of oppressing her.

119. The Afflictions of Margaret Rule

'Twas upon the Lord's day, the 10th of September, in the year 1693, that Margaret Rule, after some hours of previous disturbance in the Public Assembly, fell into odd fits, which caused her friends to carry her home, where her fits in a few hours grew into a figure that satisfied the spectators of their being preternatural. Some of the neighbours were forward enough to suspect the rise of this mischief in a house hard-by, where lived a miserable woman who had been formerly imprisoned on the suspicion of witchcraft, and who had frequently cured very painful hurts by muttering over them certain charms, which I shall not endanger the poisoning of my reader by repeating.

This woman had, the evening before Margaret fell into her calamities, very bitterly treated her and threatened her. But the hazard of hurting a poor woman that might be innocent, notwithstanding surmises that might have been more strongly grounded than those, caused the pious people in the vicinity to try rather whether incessant supplication to God alone might not procure a quicker and safer ease to the afflicted than hasty persecution of any supposed criminal. And accordingly that unexceptionable course was all that was ever followed. Yea (which I looked on as a token for good), the afflicted family was as averse as any of us all to entertain thoughts of any other course.

The young woman was assaulted by eight cruel specters, whereof she imagined that she knew three or four, but the rest came still with their faces covered, so that she could never have a distinguishing view of the countenances of those whom she thought she knew. She was very careful of my reiterated charges to forbear blazing the names, lest any good person should come to suffer any blast of reputation through the cunning malice of the great Accuser.

Nevertheless, having since privately named them to myself, I will venture to say this of them, that they are a sort of wretches who for these many years have gone under as violent presumption of witchcraft as perhaps any creature yet living upon earth, although I am far from thinking that the visions of this young woman were evidence enough to prove them so . . .

Her tormenters made *my* image to appear before her, and then made themselves masters of her tongue so far that she began in her fits to complain that I threatened her and molested her, though when she came out of them she owned that they could not so much as make my dead shape do her any harm, and that they put a force upon her tongue in her exclamations. Her greatest outcries when she was herself were for my poor prayers to be concerned on her behalf . . . .

I think I may without vanity pretend to have read not a few of the best systems of physic that have been yet seen in these American regions, but I must confess that I have never yet learned the name of the natural distemper whereto these odd symptoms do belong. However I might suggest perhaps many a natural medicine which could be of singular use against many of them.

* * *

I do testify that I have seen Margaret Rule in her afflictions from the invisible world lifted up from her bed, wholly by an invisible force, a great way towards the top of the room where she lay. In her being so lifted she had no assistance from any use of her own arms or hands or any other part of her body, not so much as her heels touching her bed or resting on any support whatsoever. And I have seen her thus lifted when not only a strong person hath thrown his whole weight across her to pull her down, but several other persons have endeavoured with all their might to hinder her from being so raised up, which I suppose that several others will testify as well as myself when called unto it.

Witness my hand.
Samuel Ames

We can also testify to the substance of what is above written, and have several times seen Margaret Rule so lifted up from her bed as that she had no use of her own limbs to help her up, but it was the declared apprehension of us, as well as others that saw it (that it was) impossible for any hands but some of the invisible world to lift her up.

Robert Earle. John Wilkins. Daniel Williams.

We whose names are underwritten do testify that one evening when we were in the chamber where Margaret Rule then lay in her late afflictions, we observed her to be by an invisible force lifted up from the bed whereon she lay, so as to touch the garret floor, while yet neither her feet nor any other part of her body rested either on the bed or any other support, but were also by the same force lifted up from all that was under her, and all this for a considerable while. We judged it several minutes, and it was as much as several of us could do with all our strength to pull her down. All which happened when there was not only we two in the chamber, but we suppose ten or a dozen more whose names we have forgotten.

Thomas Thornton.

William Hudson testifies to the substance of Thornton's testimony, to which he also hath set his hand.

—*More Wonders of the Invisible World*

* * *

> *But the tide ebbed. The reaction, the recrimination, and the appeals for restitution of property were still to come. Some of the afflicted girls went off to Boston where, on no particular authority, they were said to have entered on a life of debauchery. Even some of the jurors repented them of what they had done.*

120. The Salem Jury's Rule

We whose names are underwritten, being in the year 1692 called to serve as jurors in court at Salem, on trial of many who were by some suspected guilty of doing acts of Witchcraft upon the bodies of sundry persons:

We confess that we ourselves were not capable to understand nor able to withstand the mysterious delusions of the Powers of Darkness and Prince of the Air, but were, for want of knowledge in ourselves and better information from others, prevailed with to take up with such evidence against the accused as on further consideration and better information we justly fear was insufficient for touching the lives of any (Deuteronomy, 17. 6),* whereby we fear we have been instrumental with others, though ignorantly and unwittingly, to bring upon ourselves and this People of the Lord the guilt of innocent blood, which sin the Lord saith in Scripture he would not pardon (2 Kings, 24. 4),† that is, we suppose, in regard of his temporal judgements.

We do therefore hereby signify to all in general (and to the surviving sufferers in especial) our deep sense of and sorrow for our errors in acting on such evidence to the condemning of any person, and do hereby declare that we justly fear we were sadly deluded and mistaken, for which we are much disquieted and distressed in our minds, and do therefore humbly beg forgiveness, first of God for Christ's sake for this our error, and pray that God would not impute the guilt of it to ourselves nor others. And we also pray that we may be considered candidly and aright by the living sufferers as being then under the power of a strong and general delusion, utterly unacquainted with and not experienced in matters of that nature.

We do heartily ask forgiveness of you all, whom we have justly offended, and do declare according to our present minds, we would none of us do such things again on such grounds for the whole world, praying you to accept of this in way of satisfaction for our offence, and that you would bless the inheritance of the Lord that He may be entreated for the Land.

Foreman, Thomas Fisk	Henry Herrick, Senior
William Fisk	John Batcheler
Thomas Fisk, Junior,	John Dane
Joseph Evelith	Thomas Perly, Senior
John Peabody	Thomas Perkins
Samuel Sayer	Andrew Eliot

—*More Wonders of the Invisible World*

---

*At the mouth of two witnesses, or three witnesses, shall he that is worthy of death be put to death; but at the mouth of one witness he shall not be put to death.

†And also for the innocent blood that he shed: for he filled Jerusalem with innocent blood; which the Lord would not pardon.

* * *

In 1706, with Ann Putnam (now a woman of twenty-six) standing in the body of the church, the Reverend Joseph Green read her confession from the pulpit, and when he had finished she acknowledged it to be hers. The great hysteria had come to an end, only to be born over and over in later times and different shapes. For if we do not hang witches today, we have our own similar, vaster crimes, and after we have done with them, we always say we are sorry.

121. Ann Putnam's Confession from the Pulpit

I desire to be humbled before God for that sad and humbling Providence that befell my father's family in the year about '92; that I, being then in my childhood, should by such a Providence of God be made an instrument for the accusing of several persons of a grievous crime, whereby their lives were taken away from them, whom now I have just grounds and good reason to believe they were innocent persons; and that it was a great delusion of Satan that deceived me in that sad time, whereby I justly fear I have been instrumental with others, though ignorantly and unwittingly, to bring upon myself and this land the guilt of innocent blood; though what was said or done by me against any person I can truly and uprightly say before God and man, I did it not out of any anger, malice or ill-will to any person, for I had no such thing against any of them; but what I did was ignorantly, being deluded by Satan.

—CHARLES WENTWORTH UPHAM
Salem Witchcraft, 2 vols., 1867

Unlike the jurors, even years afterward Ann could not admit responsibility. Satan was at the root both for the deluded and for the innocent hanged.